New Wine New Wineskins

Foreword by Olu Brown

How African American Congregations
Can Reach New Generations

F. Douglas Powe Jr.

Abingdon Press / *Nashville*

NEW WINE NEW WINESKINS
HOW AFRICAN AMERICAN CONGREGATIONS
CAN REACH NEW GENERATIONS

Copyright © 2012 by Abingdon Press

This book is printed on acid-free paper.

Library of Congress Cataloging-in-Publication Data

Powe, F. Douglas.
   New wine, new wineskins : how African American congregations can reach new generations / F. Douglas Powe, Jr.
      p. cm.
   Includes bibliographical references (p.   ).
   ISBN 978-1-4267-4222-4 (book—pbk. / trade pbk. : alk. paper)
   1. Church work with African American youth. 2. Church work with youth. I. Title.
BV4468.2.A34P68 2012
259.089'96073—dc23

2011046931

12 13 14 15 16 17 18 19 20 21—10 9 8 7 6 5 4 3 2 1

MANUFACTURED IN THE UNITED STATES OF AMERICA

To my son, Frederick Douglas Powe, III,

who will experience African American Christianity

in ways his parents never imagined.

ACKNOWLEDGMENTS

I want to thank the Rev. Jeff Jaekley, who read and provided insightful comments on every chapter in the book. This project would not have been possible without his hard work.

CONTENTS

Foreword vii
Introduction xi
Chapter One—Shifting Culture 1
    The Silent Generation
    The Boomer Generation
    The Thirteenth Generation
    The Millennial Generation
    The Civil Rights Generation
    The Black Consciousness Generation
    The Integrationist Generation
    The Hip Hop Generation
    Wineskins
Chapter Two—Old Wineskins 25
    Crossroads
    Assumptions
    Epicenter
    Shaped Reality
    Vision
    Crossroads
Chapter Three—New Wineskins 45
    Space
    Seen and Heard
    Spiritual Empowerment
    Trinitarian Model
Chapter Four—New Wine 67
    Impact
    Invitation
    Ignite
    New Wine
Chapter Five—A Better Wineskin 85
    Getting Started
    Having Faith
    Making Space: Preparing a Place at the Table
    Engaging the Community
    Keeping It Real
    Making Space: Outsiders Become Insiders
    Markers
Conclusion 105
Notes 109
Study Guide 113

FOREWORD

New Wine New Wineskins is a dynamic and thought-provoking text shaped by a person who is committed to the hope that churches can be revitalized and live out their God-given mission. Douglas captures what many churches are facing, especially predominantly African American churches, in the twenty-first century. Somehow, most industries and organizations in our world have seen the need and have moved into this new century headfirst. Surprisingly, the Church world still exists somewhere between the fourteenth and fifteenth centuries while trying to reach a current generation.

If this description happens to fit your church, there is hope for you and your congregation through this wonderful book. Douglas clearly lays out the dilemma of the current state of African American congregations, along with the real and imagined obstacles blocking them from achieving God's greatest potential. Specifically, Douglas challenges congregations to become missional and vital so that contextual ministry and outreach are at the forefront of a church's priority list.

In chapter 1 you are challenged to see your church in a new way. Ultimately, you can begin to hear God's voice anew as you seek the next thing for your church. Through these inspiring pages Douglas sets the stage by reminding each of us that we are speaking to various types of people who are products of their generations. It is the church's responsibility to ensure that we do not become complacent, speaking only to one generation, but stretch outside of our comfort zones to reach all those described by Douglas in the "Civil Rights, Black Consciousness, Integrationist, and Hip Hop generations." If your church is comfortable where it is, this book may not be for you.

Chapter 2 encourages African American congregations to view themselves in relationship to the world around them. Historically these great institutions of faith have been able to recount the stories and victories of the past, stories such as being pioneers of social and human rights. Even though these victories never leave the memories of those who lived through them, there are new generations of people who do not know the story fully and in some instances may not wholly appreciate the achievements of their elders.

Hope for all African American churches is explored in chapter 3, as they dare to walk through the painful, and sometimes frightening, process of reexamining theology and practice. Douglas does not suggest that we replace the old with the new. Rather he suggests that the African American church reclaim the powerful message of justice, hope, and love. Then the church can open its doors wide to create space for varying generations to speak to, be heard by, and participate in their faith communities in new and meaningful ways.

Chapter 4 inspires the reader to rethink the way churches operate in order to let the world outside of their doors know they are open for business. Sadly, many churches are Sunday morning country clubs that offer special privileges to members only. If congregations are going to meet new people with the love of Christ, the church has to be willing to tear down the walls of tradition and membership to make all people feel welcomed and loved. Douglas mentions that "new wine represents the new mindset that is needed to rethink evangelistic practices." To reach new people we have to think new thoughts.

In the final chapter Douglas places the responsibility and inspiration to change in the lap of the reader and the congregation. He writes, "Congregations have to change and be agents of change." This eye-opening statement helps each of us realize that it is ultimately our responsibility to lead our churches through change with the help of the Holy Spirit. In fact, the entire book will cause all readers to reflect on their current commitment to the process of "reclaiming God's mission." Douglas continually prompts us that each of our churches has a mission from God to move beyond our comfort zones and walls to reach a world in need of Christ.

I am grateful for the inspiration in the pages of this book and I am inspired by the challenge it offers. As you read this wonderful book, open your heart to the movement of God's Spirit and all the new possibilities for your church.

Olu Brown

INTRODUCTION

As Pastor Downs called the meeting to order, looks of disappointment and weariness were on many faces. The church had tried three different evangelism programs in the past three years, and they still were losing members. An elderly member spoke up, "Pastor, do you have any more brilliant ideas? You told us if we were friendly that folk would come to the church." Another member quickly added, "Yeah! You told us that starting a new contemporary service would attract young people!"

Pastor Downs sighed. Those were not exactly the words spoken, but the pastor understood the members' frustration. The church remained basically the same, even though they had tried the latest evangelism program three years ago. Truth be told, they halfheartedly embraced the evangelism programs, and what they called "evangelism" was speaking to visitors in a friendly manner during fellowship time. The contemporary service looked just like the regular service, except that it featured a praise team instead of a choir. Nothing had really changed, and that was why the congregation continued to struggle.

Does this story sound familiar? More and more African American congregations are facing a crisis in today's culture. Many of these congregations are out of touch with the shifting culture and are trying everything they can to keep the doors of the church open. These congregations are living in the past while the world moves forward at the speed of light. What is often most troubling for these congregations is their inability to reach the post–civil rights generations. These congregations cannot figure out why their status quo is preventing them from growing and reaching new people for Christ.

Here's an important insight: Simply making surface changes is no longer going to work if you want your church to thrive! The question is, *How do churches really look in the mirror and see who they are?* More precisely, *How do African American churches become missional and not simply congregations with a mission?* The difference is that a missional congregation is not self-absorbed. It is not a congregation with a misinformed understanding of mission, which focuses on only maintaining that particular congregation. Although this book focuses on what it means for African American congregations to become missional, it is written in such a way that others interested in thinking deeply about evangelism in the midst of cultural change can eavesdrop on the conversation.

Until recently most African American congregations have been immune to ongoing cultural shifts, because the black church has historically been the epicenter of the African American community. It is a new day, however, and African American congregations are experiencing their own shift between the Civil Rights era and the post–Civil Rights era. This is a shift that African American congregations cannot ignore because many black churches are losing vitality and declining numerically, even while trying to be in ministry to the community.

The African American church, once considered the bedrock of the community, is no longer on the radar for many individuals.

During the Civil Rights era many African American churches were able to impact and often transform the lives of those inside and outside of the congregation. This is no longer true, particularly among the post–civil rights generations. The problem is that many African American congregations are still working with evangelistic assumptions from the Civil Rights era. These assumptions cause many African American congregations to be out of touch with those not in the church and, as a result, these congregations struggle to embody the gospel in a way that will transform the lives of individuals or the community. The evangelistic crisis they face is their inability to embody the good news of Jesus the Christ in a way that speaks to those in post–civil rights generations.

Addressing the evangelistic crisis in African American congregations will not be easy. Many African American congregations are working with old assumptions that perpetuate evangelistic practices from generations past. The assumptions of these congregations are like old wineskins, and attempting to introduce new evangelistic practices is like trying to pour new wine into an old wineskin. Jesus tells his disciples you cannot put new wine into old wineskins because the old wineskins will burst (Matthew 9:17). Jesus continues, "No one pours new wine into old wineskins. . . . Instead, people pour new wine into new wineskins so that both are kept safe." This is a familiar text that talks about the problem of compatibility. Jesus suggests that it is not possible to put the new wine into the old wineskin because something happens when the two come together that creates a mess—the old wineskin gives way—it explodes as the new wine ferments.

Naming the assumptions of many African American congregations as old wineskins is a way to understand how evangelistic ideas are framed in these churches. These congregations continue trying to pour new evangelistic practices into an old framework. Trying to process new wine in an old wineskin is not fruitful.[1]

The assumptions held by these congregations are grounded in the experiences of a previous generation to which current generations no longer relate. Some of the old assumptions are slowly disintegrating, but these congregations continue to believe the problem is not them and point the finger elsewhere. The finger is usually pointed in one of three directions.

☞ First, the finger points toward new evangelistic practices. Those maintaining the old assumptions argue there is no need for new practices because it was the old practices that built the church. The reality is that those holding to old assumptions want the new practices to be consistent with their ideals and traditions. This means using the same idioms, language, and affirmations that sustain the old wineskin. Thus new ideas are not able to flourish because of a mentality that negates anything new.

Many African American congregations fail to attract new parishioners because those operating with an old-wineskin mentality are stuck in a particular cultural box. For example, some congregations continue to perceive the community around them from a 1960s mentality and continue to do ministry from that point of reference. A 1990s Hip Hop artist, Phife Dawg, captures this mentality when he raps, "How can a reverend preach, when a rev can't define the music of our youth?"[2]

Whether it is a generational gap, economic gap, or class gap, those with the old-wineskin mentality are not connecting with the post–civil rights generations. These congregations think they have tried to do evangelism, but they have only succeeded in further alienating those in the community.

☞ Second, the finger points toward those individuals coming in and upsetting the applecart. When new parishioners join the congregation, it often causes an "us versus them" mentality because they bring different assumptions with them. Many of the current members, perpetuating the old wineskin, want the new parishioners only if they understand "the way we do things here." The truth is that some members are so beholden to the old wineskin that they would rather disintegrate completely than consider new ideas that may transform the congregation. The goal is to maintain the way things were, with no consideration given to being influenced by those who better understand the culture.

This is why many congregations simply reach out to others just like themselves. Congregations involved in this ploy are deceiving themselves by thinking they are engaging in new evangelistic practices, when in reality the goal is to disciple those already like them. Churches with this attitude are not shifting their assumptions or developing new evangelistic practices. They are pouring the same wine into the same old wineskin. Individuals may be new to the church, but they are only accepted if they fit the old mold that has existed for years at the congregation. In these congregations the good news is not gospel-centered; it is egocentric because the goal is to maintain homogeneity.

☞ Third, the finger points toward those with more resources. Those with an old-wineskin mentality start blaming their struggles on the fact that they have limited resources in comparison to other congregations. These congregations are implying that if they had the same resources, then they would flourish. Certainly resources are important, but they **do not** guarantee success.

For example, starting a contemporary service or adding a new worship time as a method of reaching out to individuals does require resources. It is my observation that the new service or new time is usually not for the benefit of those outside of the congregation, but for those inside the congregation. These churches are trying to pour new wine into the same old wineskin. These congregations do not necessarily understand the Holy Spirit as empowering them to live out transformed lives in the culture, because their focus is on internal changes that satisfy their spiritual cravings. The issue is not simply resources, but developing a new mindset within the current congregation that shifts the way they think about and approach evangelism.

To be fair, all of these strategies have worked and are working to increase membership (assuming increased membership is the goal) for some churches, but for how long? The real question is, **Which one, two, or three of these fingers point to scenarios that fit your congregation?** Are you ready to do something about it?

Many African American churches are dying because congregations perpetuate an old-wineskin mentality. They have fallen into the same snare as other declining congregations who are no longer missional. They continue to hang on to an old-wineskin mentality, hoping to find a silver lining in the sky. The reality is that none of these approaches deal with the cultural shift that many congregations have ignored and continue to ignore. By continuing to ignore cultural shifts, African American congregations run the risk of not only decline, but eventual death.

A new approach is required that understands the cultural shifts occurring while maintaining the integrity of the gospel. In order to successfully apply a new approach, African American congregations will have to develop new wineskins. A new approach requires changing the evangelistic assumptions still haunting some congregations. New assumptions will transform the way churches adapt to cultural shifts. Ultimately, a new approach involves altering the way many African American congregations are worshiping and reaching out into the community.

Some African American churches are doing this by changing their practices and attempting to create a more hospitable church or by developing more passionate worship. These practices are critical for congregations, but by themselves they do not translate into making new wineskins. If the DNA of the congregation has not been transformed, then altering the practices will not engender real change. For example, a congregation can devote a lot of energy into being more hospitable in the hopes of attracting more members. This practice assumes two things. First, it assumes that people are actually visiting the church and seeking to join. A congregation can be the friendliest place in town; but if no one is visiting or if the church has limited visibility, the potential for numerical growth is limited. Second, the hospitality must extend to all people and not just those "suitable for membership." Many congregations are friendly but, depending on economic status, race, or political views, the degree of friendliness varies.

The question is, *What is necessary for a church to make new wineskins?* Developing new practices is an important part of making new wineskins, but it is also necessary to think deeper about the assumptions behind many of those practices. We are constantly hammering congregants over the head with the need for growth and getting them involved in programs intended to help the church grow, but often to no avail. Typically churches move from program to program, trying different practices in hopes of finding the pot of gold at the end of the rainbow.

What if the problem is not the practices but the assumptions behind the practices? This is not an excuse to stop engaging in important evangelistic practices—most congregations can improve dramatically in this area—*but it recognizes that the evangelistic challenge most churches face cannot be resolved by practices alone.*

This book offers African American congregations a way of moving forward to create new wineskins capable of holding and sustaining new wine. It does this by reclaiming a missional understanding for evangelism in the African American community. The evangelistic innovativeness and influence of African American congregations should be their ongoing commitment to share the good news of salvation in the community. If African American congregations frame evangelism in this missional manner, then practices like hospitality and testimony are transformed because the DNA of the congregation has been altered. Resolving the evangelistic crisis facing many African American congregations will not be easy or accomplished overnight. Reevaluating the current congregational assumptions framing evangelism in many African American congregations is a step in the right direction.

This book has five chapters that will engage African American congregations and those interested in altering the DNA of an old wineskin. Chapter 1 ("Shifting Culture") describes the shifts that have occurred within African American culture over the last fifty years and why these shifts are important for the way we understand church. Chapter 2 ("Old Wineskins") outlines the challenges faced by declining African American congregations. This chapter focuses on the old wineskins and the current evangelistic framework used by many African American congregations and others with a similar theological bent. Chapter 3 ("New Wineskins") argues for reclaiming a missional theology for evangelism. This chapter uses various resources to develop an evangelistic theology that promotes sharing the good news with those in the community. Chapter 4 ("New Wine") discusses the opportunities for evangelism in a shifting culture. This chapter examines some of the new assumptions (such as, authentic leadership, collaboration, and meaningful spirituality) structuring our shifting culture and the opportunity for developing a new evangelistic framework. Chapter 4 helps older congregations move beyond us-versus-them mentalities. Chapter 5 ("A Better Wineskin") focuses on developing new evangelistic practices that will help these congregations engage the cultural shift in a way that maintains integrity for older members and invites new members to participate. This chapter emphasizes creating a different ethos in the congregation that engenders vitality.

It is time African American congregations examined the assumptions behind their evangelistic practices and developed a new framework that reconnects congregations and ultimately the community to the love of God through Jesus the Christ.

CHAPTER 1
SHIFTING CULTURE

It was youth Sunday! Mother Brown was frowning because only five youth showed up to participate. She heard the Sunday school teacher going over their lines for the program that would start in five minutes. Mother Brown stopped Sister Carmen and asked, "Where is your daughter's family?" Sister Carmen replied, "She did not want to come. Talking nonsense that our youth program has not changed since she was a child." Sister Carmen walked away shaking her head.

Mother Brown watched her go toward the kitchen, but the words stuck in her head, "the youth program has not changed!" Mother Brown had been at the church forty years and the truth was the youth program had not changed. She didn't see why it needed to change. Mother Brown shook her head and said softly, "I just don't get this new generation!"

How many times have you heard or said, "I just do not get this new generation!" What is going on in the African American culture that is so different from ten, twenty, or forty years ago? There are several possibilities for approaching the shifting culture in the African American community. My approach is rethinking some of the generational categories developed by Strauss and Howe in *Generations*.[1] They develop eighteen generational categories in their book, but my focus is on four of their categories (Silent, Boomer, 13er, and Millennial).[2] Strauss and

Howe use a cross-section of the United States to highlight trends and characteristics of generations. What is lost in this approach is some of the subtlety related to particular trends in the African American community. This is especially true concerning the importance of personal and communal faith for African Americans.

It is important to understand the cultural shifts within the African American community, because it will give us new insights into how congregations have to think differently about the African American church and evangelism, and it points out some important differences between those active during the Civil Rights era and post–civil rights generations. Understanding these differences aids us in developing a new vision that will alter the way we think and do evangelism.

Let me begin with a quick summary of Strauss and Howe's development of the four generational categories (Silent, Boomer, 13er, and Millennial) and their importance for American culture. Second, I will re-define these categories to address the generational shifts within the African American community. Last, I will offer some closing comments on what all of this means for congregations seeking to be missional.

THE SILENT GENERATION

The dates for those born during the Silent generation are between 1925 and 1942.[3] Strauss and Howe quote Frank Conroy, who claims, "We had no leaders, no program, no sense of our own power, and no culture exclusively of our own."[4] The point is this generation had little voice and did not produce leaders or change American culture significantly. In fact, Strauss and Howe categorize this generation as adaptive because of their ability to fit in and not be in the forefront.

The challenge within American culture for the Silent generation is they are born after World War I's G.I.s and before the Boomers. They are the ultimate sandwich.[5] Silents adapt either to those who come before them or those coming after. A few of the famous Anglo Silents are Clint Eastwood, Marilyn Monroe, and Phil Donahue.[6] Noticeably absent from this generation is someone who became president of the United States. This is a part of the rationale by Strauss and Howe for arguing this is a silent generation in terms of high-profile leadership.

It is interesting, however, that this generation produced most of the Civil Rights leaders.[7] Yet, very little attention is given to the dramatic impact these leaders had on American culture and specifically African American culture. In fact, Strauss and Howe argue, "Silent appeals for change have seldom arisen from power or fury, but rather through a self-conscious humanity and tender social conscience ('Deep in my heart, I do believe/We shall overcome someday')."[8] The implication is that African Americans were not furious with on-going racial conditions in the U.S. I agree that those within the Civil Rights movement had to raise the consciousness of the nation, but this does not discount a deep sense of anger over the conditions faced by the African American community.

THE BOOMER GENERATION

Boomers were born between 1943 and 1960.[9] As a group they are idealists because of their experience as youth.[10] Boomers are the children of the G.I.s and inherit a different American culture

3

than the Silent generation who lived during WWII.[11] A few famous Anglo Boomers are Oliver North, Donald Trump, and Jane Pauley.

Strauss and Howe describe Boomers as self-absorbed and dependent on their own instincts.[12] The focus is on what I can achieve as an individual. Donald Trump is a prototypical Boomer because of his emphasis on being a self-made individual who can tackle anything. This focus on the self causes a spiritual rift within this generation between those who are more New Age and those who are evangelical.[13] Both sides are bound to their particular absolutes and idealism. Within the Boomer generation intense debates over issues like the right to life are not uncommon.

What is missing from the analysis is the impact of race during the turbulent formative years of the Boomer generation. Many of the first wave of Boomers experienced the Civil Rights movement firsthand, but Strauss and Howe offer no real insight into how this impacted their lives. In their section entitled "Coming of Age," the emphasis is on Boomer activism related to the "Free Speech Movement."[14] While this captures some of the upheaval of the late sixties, it misses the mark of integrating the turmoil experienced by all generations during the Civil Rights movement.

THE THIRTEENTH GENERATION

The Thirteenth generation does not even have a real name. The dates for this generation are 1961–81. Strauss and Howe categorize this generation as reactive. In part, they point to *Washington Post* writer Nancy Smith's phrase, "the generation after," as indicative of why this generation is nameless.[15] The

Thirteenth generation is the one always coming along after life-changing events like Woodstock, Watergate, etc.[16] A few famous Anglo Thirteeners are Tom Cruise, Brooke Shields, and Tatum O'Neal. The point is not that this generation missed these events, but that as a generation they contributed nothing.

In fact, Strauss and Howe quote Felicity Barringer, who writes an unflattering description of the Thirteeners as "a lost generation, an army of aging Bart Simpsons, possibly armed and dangerous."[17] The implication is this generation has not turned out the way it should. Strauss and Howe point to declining academic performance and the perception that this generation is not that bright to reinforce the Bart Simpson analogy.[18] Not only is this generation nameless, it is a day late and a dollar short and certainly not the sharpest knife in the drawer! These are harsh critiques leveled against a generation that lived during the post–Civil Rights era.

What is missing from Strauss and Howe's analysis is the fact that the racial landscape changed significantly during this time because of the Civil Rights movement. This is the first generation to deal with busing and integration on a national scale. They offer no analysis of the battles over busing and neighborhood integration.

THE MILLENNIAL GENERATION

The Millennial generation starts in 1982 for Strauss and Howe. This generation gets its name in part from the fact that they are the historic generation that came into their own in the twenty-first century. A few of the famous Millennials are Danica Patrick, Dylan and Cole Sprouse, and Miley Cyrus. Strauss and Howe understand this generation as a new beginning in America as a result of stronger parental control. One example of this is the attempt not to repeat perceived mistakes made with Thirteeners—like creating a latchkey family.[19]

These parental controls have made Millennials civic-minded. Strauss and How argue that the goal of this generation is living with civic virtues like "community and cooperation."[20] This shift is reflected in the movies entertainment studios like Disney are making for Millennials; they differ from those made for Thirteeners, which focused on "individualism and difference."[21] This generation will benefit from a greater adult oversight and not be left on their own.[22]

Strauss and Howe argue that the early 1980s marked a move in America toward promoting "quality education" in public schools.[23] They point to tangible things like report cards for school districts and increased pay for teachers.[24] Unfortunately these facts do not differentiate between suburban, rural, and urban schools. Because of a greater tax base and more parental involvement, middle class school districts can afford to pay teachers more and usually rank higher in statistical categories. Deteriorating urban and rural school districts are constantly trying to stay afloat, attract teachers, and encourage parental involvement. While the picture Strauss and Howe proposes for Millennials is helpful, it still neglects some of the pertinent shifts in American culture. What is missing from their analysis is the intensifying of the class divide during the Millennial generation. It is important to acknowledge the impact of class when thinking about community and what that means for various segments of the population. African American and other children who lived in suburban areas probably benefited from many of the shifts presented by Strauss and Howe in ways that those in declining areas did not. From our twenty-first-century perspective, we now know that class issues have tremendously impacted America and particularly African American families.

From this quick analysis of Strauss and Howe, we get a picture of some generational trends in America. In part, we get a glimpse of how each generation buys into and constructs the American dream.[25] For example, according to Strauss and Howe, Boomers tore down and reconstructed the American dream on their own terms, but the Thirteeners were never quite able to live into the American dream in some important ways. The ability or inability of each generation to live out the American dream leaves a mark not only on their generation, but on those that follow. Strauss and Howe call these marks "generational endowments."[26] They develop these generational endowments in a particular way that focuses on peer personalities and the "lifecycle of each generation type."[27]

I like the language of generational endowments, but I use the term differently as I explore African American generational categories. The question is, "What endowments have each African American generation passed along to the next that have shaped and continue to shape black culture?" This question is particularly pertinent for African American church culture. This book will answer this question by developing African American generational categories that are both inclusive of and counterparts to the Strauss and Howe paradigms.

THE CIVIL RIGHTS GENERATION

I date this generation between 1921 and 1940. This is a little different from the dates for the Silent generation, which are from

1925 to 1942. A few of the prominent African Americans born during this time were Martin Luther King, Jr., Malcom X, Maya Angelou, and Diane Nash. Obviously, each of these figures played a prominent role in the Civil Rights movement. Contrary to Strauss and Howe, who categorized the Silent generation as adaptive, it is more appropriate for African Americans to name this generation "the change agents."

This generation called into question the then-popular interpretation of the American dream and organized to enact changes that are still embedded within American culture. Floyd-Thomas argues that the Civil Rights movement (this generation) worked to endow African Americans with freedom and dignity.[28] Significantly, this freedom and dignity is not simply individualistic, but it's a freedom and dignity that also challenges Anglo Americans to reinterpret the American dream.

While Strauss and Howe highlight attempts to alter the consciousness of Americans through non-violent means by African Americans, they do not pick up on the fury that fueled the non-violence. King's "Letter from a Birmingham Jail" is an example of African American anger over the racial conditions confronting blacks while still trying to raise the consciousness of those Anglo Americans who argued that African Americans were moving too fast and should wait. This generation was tired of waiting and sought to transform the very fabric of American culture.

What is fascinating about this generation is that many of the leaders were religious and the fact that they shaped African American religiosity for decades. For African American Christians, important organizations like the SCLC (Southern Christian Leadership Conference) were birthed during this time. In fact, when many African Americans talk about black leadership, most of the names are from the Civil Rights generation. The ability of the cadre of these leaders to impact the religious, political, and social fabric of America has not been duplicated.[29]

The social fabric of the country experienced a transformation process that, in many ways, is still an on-going project. The Civil Rights generation challenged all Americans to envision a nation where race and ethnicity were not determining factors or limiting factors for rights. Although it is hard for many younger people to imagine, it is because of the Civil Rights generation that African and Anglo Americans can drink from the same water fountain, eat in the same restaurants, use the same restroom facility, etc., in many states. These are just a few examples of how the social fabric changed because of this generation.

Brown vs. The Board of Education is a landmark case in education rights for African Americans. The idea of separate but equal schools was a fallacy. Because social norms prevented most African Americans from living in Anglo American school districts, many African American schoolchildren in the North and South used outdated textbooks and did not have the resources of their Anglo American counterparts. The Civil Rights generation challenged this intentional undermining of educational opportunities in the United States. The goal was to provide an equal opportunity for all children to prosper intellectually.

Politically this is one of the most active times in American history for African Americans, and most of the political leaders came out of organized religion. One could not easily separate spirituality and politics within the African American community. Many of these leaders were able to integrate biblical language with rhetoric from documents like the Constitution to prick the American consciousness. The goal was not simply political activism aimed at constructing a new power base, but moving the United States toward a higher understanding of humanity that embodied the founding documents that this country claims as "holy."

Because of the connection between politics and religion for this generation, it is no surprise that the embodiment of political activism often occurred in local congregations. Many of the marches started at churches and many of the meetings were held in local congregations, because the church house was a focal point for the African American community. The Civil Rights generation strongly believed that their success was ensured because they were spiritually grounded.

Being spiritually grounded meant that they understood how social, educational, political, and religious ideals all shape who we are as individuals. The Christian leaders of this generation were able to construct a spirituality that moved individuals toward wholeness and not disembodiment. The church was the place where one could truly experience holiness and wholeness because it addressed one's entire existence and sought to transform that existence. It is no wonder that many African American congregations grew during this time.

The endowments of this generation are many, and books have been written on their impact on American culture. Let me highlight three of these endowments that are important for African American culture and particularly black congregations. First, this generation created a model of black male leadership in the church and outside of it that continues to be paradigmatic today.[30] This generation developed a model of leadership in the church and politics that, until recently, placed the pastor in the center of both arenas. The expectation in the African American community was (and is, to some extent) that the pastor (usually male) will not only lead the congregation, but is to be the voice of the African American community. Even today, anyone running for office who wants the support of the African American community makes it a point to visit black congregations, because they understand this is where the power base was in the community.

Second, this generation believed the church played an instrumental role in constructing the beloved community. The theological way to express this is that this generation believed the church could make the kingdom of God a reality within American culture. The church believed that by participating in the Civil Rights movement, it was creating a new society that radically altered race relations. The church was not only a place for personal transformation, but a place where the structures of society were altered. The goal was to alter the structures in such a way that the divisions between black and white would become meaningless.

Third, this generation redefined black identity. Blackness was no longer equated with second rate, but embodied true American citizenship. In his speech "The American Dream," King argued that African Americans must live as full citizens even while experiencing oppression.[31] African American identity is not defined by others, but is defined by how we perceive ourselves.[32] This way of thinking about black identity was reinforced in the African American church. It was in the church that African Americans often rallied before marches, reminding themselves of their citizenship and right to participate in the American dream.

These generational endowments continue to shape American culture and black congregations. The Civil Rights generation in many ways is the most important because of the legacy it created. But the key question regarding this generation is, **"Are African Americans still interpreting these generational endowments through a 1950s and 60s lens?"** This is the question that will frame the next chapter.

THE BLACK CONSCIOUSNESS GENERATION

The dates for this generation are 1941 to 1960. Those in this generation are re-definers because they were committed to black empowerment. This generation builds off of the Civil Rights generation by emphasizing the beauty of blackness. A few African Americans born during this time are Jeremiah Wright, H. Rapp Brown, Jesse Jackson, and Angela Davis. These individuals and others like them shifted from a strong emphasis on interracial cooperation to black empowerment.[33]

This shift is both sociological and theological. Sociologically the Black Panther Party and other pro-black organizations articulated the political and economic demands of many African Americans using rhetoric that was more demanding than nuanced. For example, the Panthers did not assert a non-violent doctrine and advocated for self-defense against police brutality.[34] They were intentional in their commitment to protecting African Americans and African American neighborhoods.

Theologically the shift was toward developing a black liberation theology. This theology emphasized the blackness of Jesus and its implications for African American congregations.[35] At this time, several African American congregations started developing their own curriculum, centering on new images and interpretations of biblical characters. The goal was to redefine what it means to be a Christian from the perspective of an African American living in the United States. The black liberation movement articulated theologically what was being said by some in the black power movement.

Many of the African American pastors (mostly male, like Jeremiah Wright and Floyd Flake) brought up during this generation were able to combine insights from the Civil Rights generation with black empowerment, enabling them to connect the church to the community in significant ways. For example, Floyd Flake has been committed to urban development for the Queens community in New York City, where his church is located, as a means of empowerment. This model of economic community development in urban centers is one that has strong roots in the Black Consciousness generation.

Sociologically and theologically, while the Black Consciousness generation shares some qualities with Boomers, there are also some important differences. The inheritance from the G.I. generation enjoyed by many Anglo Boomers was never fully enjoyed by African Americans because they were still coming of age during the racial wars. The shifts in religion many Boomers experienced were not as pronounced in the African American community, especially the Christian community, because the church was still the focal point. For example, the Black Consciousness generation did not (for the most part) experience the New Age versus evangelical split.

Sociologically and theologically the Black Consciousness generation continued to build on what they inherited from the Civil Rights generation, and they also passed along three important endowments to the next generation. First, the Black Consciousness generation was interested in deepening our understanding of blackness in a way that continues to inform citizenship. The construction of black identity started during the Civil Rights generation is not abandoned, but it is focused in a way that promotes black empowerment. The goal is not simply citizenship, but redefining the black community.

Second, the Black Consciousness generation deepened our understanding of the systemic nature of social ills. While the Civil Rights generation envisioned society moving toward the beloved community, the Black Consciousness generation helped us understand the challenges of making the beloved community a reality. The perspective of many within the Black Consciousness generation was that the beloved community cannot simply be a recapitulation of the current societal structures, with the only change being that African Americans now have civil rights, because this would mean, economically and politically, that nothing had really changed.

Third, the Black Consciousness generation understood the important connection between politics, economic development, and the church. The Civil Rights generation focused on politics and the church. The benefit of coming along a generation later was that some of the pastors within the Black Consciousness generation were able to incorporate economic development as a means of empowerment for the community surrounding the church. Sociologically and theologically this generation built on what it inherited by addressing some of the social ills facing many African American neighborhoods. Hence the key question regarding this generation is, **"Has economic development become a code word for prosperity ministry that benefits only a few?"**

THE INTEGRATIONIST GENERATION

The dates for this generation are 1961 to 1980. This generation recently made history with the election of the first African
American president, Barack Obama. This generation is oppor-
tunistic because it inherited a legacy from the two previous generations that allowed for social, educational, political, and
religious mobility not typically afforded to previous African
Americans. A few of the African Americans born during this
generation are Barack Obama, Tupac, Jill Scott, and Erykah
Badu. These individuals represent the changing face of America
and the African American community as it lives into the suc-
cesses of the previous generations.

Socially this is the first generation that lived in what were previously Anglo neighborhoods. This shift in the housing patterns
caused three discernable trends. First, white flight by Anglo
Americans not wanting to live near African Americans, but usually done under the guise of concern for property values. Second,
integrated neighborhoods created a new diversity rarely experienced in America previously. But third, the shift fractured the
African American community, creating a divide between those
who "got out" and those who still lived in predominantly
depressed African American areas.

This changing social pattern in American culture, especially
for African Americans, reshaped the landscape by both reinforc-
ing racial tensions and tearing down some walls. White flight
affirmed for many African Americans the belief that Anglo
Americans were racially prejudiced and wanted nothing to do
with them. Conversely, truly integrated neighborhoods did
provide opportunities for the races to mingle in ways previously

discouraged and did free neighbors to discover commonalities.[36] In fact, economic bonds creating class cohesion between some blacks and whites started to become normative. Some African Americans started believing class was more important than race in America and did not necessarily understand the relationship between the two.[37]

In terms of education this generation was the first to experience busing. One of the reasons for naming this generation Integrationist is because of busing. Busing students was a legal solution to resolve educational inequities between the races and create more integrated schools. It is also important to note that a shift also took place at the collegiate level, with more African American students going to majority Anglo schools. While this shift did promote integration, it continues to have a negative economic impact on some historically black colleges.

Because of the social shifts in American culture during the Integrationist generation, a similar observation about the relationship between race and class can be made concerning education. One of the ways around busing for Anglo Americans and African Americans with means was to move out of those areas where students were bused. The idea of creating stronger schools often did not materialize because of white flight and because African Americans who were upwardly mobile left the school systems where busing was the norm. Not only race but class was an issue because huge economic discrepancies still existed in the educational system.

The political scene shifted for this generation, because most Integrationists grew up thinking African American politicians were the norm. The election of Carl Stokes as mayor in Cleveland and the election of other African American political officials at the local level, once considered radical, became normative. The sense of struggle that enabled African Americans to run for and hold political offices started to become only a memory for this generation. While they were not completely dislocated from the Civil Rights and Black Consciousness generations, the success of those generations created a disconnect for many Integrationists.

Because of the social, educational, and political shifts occurring in the culture, the religious landscape also began to shift because the African American church was no longer the *de facto* center of the community. Upwardly mobile African Americans started driving back into neighborhoods they had left to go to church. Even today, many of these individuals lose all connections to the community and only stay a few hours on Sunday for worship. Some of these churches have ceased being neighborhood congregations and have become invisible within the communities where they are located.

Another significant change occurred during the second wave of the Integrationist generation: the idea of someone having spirituality but not necessarily being connected to one particular religion. Some of the neo-soul artists like Erykah Badu reinforce this way of thinking about spirituality. Whereas a couple of decades earlier it was a safe assumption to connect African American spirituality to Christianity or Islam, with the second wave of Integrationists, this is not the case. This further de-centered the church as the institution that creates meaning in the African American community, specifically spiritual meaning.

The Integrationists are a landmark generation for African Americans because significant racial and class shifts occurred in the culture. Strauss and Howe read this generation more as a transitional generation to Millennials. For African Americans, however, this generation leaves a legacy that changes the contour of African American culture and American culture.

The endowments from this generation intensified the class divide within the African American community. The Integrationists are the first generation to really experience social and educational integration on a broad scale. Those with means within the African American community have choices that were not available to previous generations. Many chose to move out of historic African American neighborhoods in order to seek a better standard of living and educational opportunities.

Some Integrationists are unique religiously because they divorce spirituality from a particular tradition. Not only are many urban congregations no longer the center of the community, but they also are not the center of one's life. This shift has implications for evangelism in the African American community because being connected to organized religion is no longer automatic. The question used to be, *Which form of organized religion?* Or more specifically for Christians, Which denomination? For Integrationists the question has become whether or not to associate with organized religion at all.

For the first time the Christian story is not necessarily "the story." It still is "the story" for most of the Civil Rights generation and even for many in the Black Consciousness generation.[38] However, during the Integrationist generation, because of all the cultural shifts, the story that held the community together started to fragment, so that many individuals forgot about its importance, did not care about its importance, or never really heard about its importance. Evangelistic practices based upon assumptions generated by the Civil Rights generation are no longer creating the holiness or wholeness that maintained healthy congregations. The key question with regard to this generation is, **"What *is* the story for this generation?"**

THE HIP HOP GENERATION

The dates for this generation are 1981–2000. The Hip Hop generation is capitalist because they focus on the economic side of the American dream. This does not mean they ignore community or refuse to use their resources to aid others, but this generation understands the importance of economics as it relates to the American dream. A few of those in this generation are Beyoncè Knowles, Serena Williams, Lebron James, and Raven Symone. These individuals are typical of others in this generation who do not set limits on their careers and are often involved in multiple careers at the same time. For example, Serena Williams is a tennis star, but she also designs and markets her own clothing line.

This generation is fascinating in the way it has continued to shift the social, educational, political, and religious landscape for African Americans. In some ways this generation, because of its capitalistic focus, has increased the divide between those with means and those without. In other ways this generation perceives the class divide in America and brings attention to it in music, fashion, etc. One of the challenges is that the very vehicles (e.g., rap music) this generation uses to shine a spotlight on the inequities in African American culture perpetuate not only the divide but misogynistic and violent messages as well. A continuing struggle within the African American community is how one can hear the truth in the message without pre-judging and closing one's ears completely to the messenger.

This challenge plays out socially in how many in this generation appear. It is not uncommon to find, both in urban and suburban centers, Hip Hop-ers walking around with loose-fitting, baggy pants and long shirts. What makes this even more fascinating is that this fashion trend is not limited to African Americans because Anglo Americans and the Latino communities have picked it up. The Hip Hop generation has influenced not only African American culture, but most of American culture in the way people dress, talk, and interact with each other.

However, a focus on economics is a two-edged sword when it comes to the divide within the African American community. On the one hand, it has connected African American urban and suburban youth by giving them a common social arena in which to exist. On the other hand, it has not diminished the divide, because fashion trends cost money and some youth are spending money trying to stay trendy. Even the African Americans creating and profiting from some of these trends, like Sean Combs (Puff Daddy), are not really a part of the communities where these products are being purchased.

Education is the one arena where the class divide is the most prevalent within the African American community. While urban and suburban youth can share a common arena socially, this is not the case when it comes to education. The divide in education can create tension between urban and suburban African Americans. Suburban African Americans are portrayed as sell-outs because they are no longer connected to African Americans still in the urban core. Urban African Americans are often portrayed as "those people." *Those people* are identified by their lack of resources and low educational achievements.

Because of the capitalistic emphasis of this generation, education often takes a backseat. For example, Lebron James, because of his skills as a basketball player, moved from high school straight to the NBA to earn a "phat" paycheck. I am not commenting on James's educational achievements or arguing in favor of the new NBA rule banning the move James made, but I am suggesting that many African American youth see the economic advantage of his move to the extent that their sole focus becomes how one can "make it."[39] Being a life-long learner has little impact for those who perceive making a lot of money as the answer to all of life's ills.

Interestingly, this generation is usually perceived as politically unimportant because they do not typically vote. One of the things that helped Obama become president was a higher turnout by those in the Hip Hop generation.[40] In terms of political impact within the African American community and American culture, it is still too early to comment on the contributions of the Hip Hop generation. We are just starting to see the political impact of the Integrationists, and it will be a while before the Hip Hop generation moves en mass into the larger political arena.

But this generation does shift the African American Christian landscape, because many are more comfortable in megacongregations that mimic a celebrity culture. One of the attractions of these congregations is the well-known senior pastor.[41] Attending such a congregation brings with it a certain status, even if most of the parishioners have no direct contact with the pastor. These congregations tend to be higher tech and make use of various media formats that have become normative for this generation. While this generation is relational, it is relational in a different way than previous generations. The Hip Hop generation does not need to know the pastor personally, but must *feel* connected to the pastor and church. This can happen via social networks or based upon the pastor's status. Many Hip Hop-ers are comfortable with an anonymous Christianity that buys into their capitalistic outlook on life.

Certainly, as with any generation, the picture I have drawn is not true for every individual in the Hip Hop generation. It is important to point out that the most significant generation missing in mainline denominations (Lutheran, Methodist, Presbyterian, etc.) is the Hip Hop-ers. While some from this generation continue to attend mainline congregations, it is a widely accepted fact that most mainline congregations are struggling to connect with others in this generation. Chapter 3 will present ideas for congregations to rethink their assumptions about the church as a means of being in dialogue with this generation. The key question with regard to this generation is, **"Are congregations willing to change their assumptions about church?"**

WINESKINS

What do wineskins have to do with cultural shifts? Is it a stretch to contemporize the analogy Jesus was making and relate it to the church? The African American church during the Civil Rights era constructed a particular paradigm of the church that was captivating and in line with the cultural shifts of that time. When the culture started shifting dramatically again during the Integrationist generation, most African American congregations were still comfortable with the Civil Rights paradigm they had embodied for years.

Fifty to sixty years later, many of these congregations are still working with the assumptions and practices of the Civil Rights generation. The fact that five to six decades later so many congregations still perceive themselves as Civil Rights churches speaks to the influence of that generation. If it were not for the Civil Rights generation, African Americans would not be where they are as a people and the church might not have been so central for so long. The reality, however, is the culture has shifted and will continue to shift, and many African American congregations cannot figure out why their old wineskins are incompatible with new wine.

These congregations face the challenge in the forthcoming years of having to look deep into themselves and be honest about the disconnect, socially, educationally, politically, and spiritually, that has been created over the past six decades. However, I want to be clear that I am *not* discounting the influence of the Civil Rights generation or arguing we should simply move forward forgetting the past. I am arguing that the evangelistic challenge facing many African American congregations is a result of not understanding the cultural shifts that have occurred post–civil rights.

These shifts have significant social, educational, political, and, most importantly, theological implications that shape how African American congregations seek to be missional. While no one book can tackle all of the issues confronting African American congregations, this book will explore the missional implications of the cultural shifts occurring in African American communities and why black congregations need to understand these shifts. Toward this end, the next chapter will discuss what made many African American congregations so attractive during the Civil Rights and Black Consciousness generations and why this picture is no longer captivating to younger generations.

REVISITING THE QUESTIONS

1. Are African Americans still interpreting these generational endowments through a 1950s and 60s lens? Do African American congregations still see the world through 1950s and 60s glasses? (page 12)

2. Has economic development become a code word for prosperity ministry that benefits only a few? Is the goal uplifting the community or the prosperity of a few? (page 14)

3. What *is* the story for this generation? How does the Hip-Hop generation define itself? (page 19)

4. Are congregations willing to change their assumptions about church? Are you willing to rethink church through new generational lenses? (page 22)

ACTIVITY

Read 1 Samuel 3:1-21—Think about Eli's response (verse 18) to hearing Samuel will be the new prophetic voice soon and then answer this question: Are we helping those in the post-civil rights generations to live out their calling?

CHAPTER 2
OLD WINESKINS

The Lord will see us through, The Lord will see us through,
We shall overcome someday.[1]

Revelation to Genesis, something you cannot dismiss
Keys to Crossroad, come to abyss![2]

Music often gives us an insight into what is happening in culture. "We Shall Overcome" is one of the most famous songs coming out of the Civil Rights era and speaks to the hopes of those inside and outside of the church in the African American community. In the early nineties a group called X-Clan released a rap entitled "Verbs of Power." They said that we need to start with the concept of a new day (think "new creation" as found in the Book of Revelation) and reverse the traditional approach of beginning with Genesis.

In some ways both musical pieces are pointing toward a different future. In another way these two pieces represent the cultural shifts taking place in society and specifically African American culture. For many African Americans during the Civil Rights era, "We Shall Overcome" spoke to a shared worldview and the hopes for shaping society in a particular way—a truly integrated citizenry.[3] Another way to name the hopes of many from the Civil Rights era is that African Americans would truly experience the American dream.

CROSSROADS

X-Clan said that after the Civil Rights era African Americans came to a crossroads and had to decide how to move forward. Integration did occur, but it has not resulted in the entire African American community experiencing the American dream. In many ways this chapter recognizes and rejoices over the accomplishments of the Civil Rights and Black Consciousness generations. It also argues that if African American congregations want to build on those accomplishments, it is time to rethink church for post–civil rights generations. The old wineskin mentality of African American congregations being the epicenter in the community, shaping the reality of the community, and having the right vision for the community are no longer fair assumptions.

It is a new time, but most African American congregations are still practicing a way of doing church that is grounded in a "We Shall Overcome" culture. I am not suggesting that a Civil Rights and Black Consciousness way of doing church is negative. Quite the contrary! This way of doing church has brought us to the crossroads and shaped black reality for decades. The question is, **"How are congregations going to move forward?"** Some congregations will argue we need to stay the course because American culture has not changed that much. I am suggesting a different course of action, one that is informed by the past, but recognizes it is time to rethink some of our assumptions.

Denial will not work! Continuing to believe that the post–civil rights generations will share the old-wineskin world-view is not working. What is needed is to understand the post–civil rights generations and why the old-wineskin mentality no longer works. Many African American congregations have to leave their comfort zone and become missional again.

The advantage for many congregations is that black churches have historically figured out how to be missional. African American congregations have historically been able to see the future in ways that other institutions have not. African American congregations have impacted the culture; they have been invitational in the way they shaped the culture; and they ignited a flame in people to move toward something new. The question is, "What is happening now?"

African American congregations are trying to impact the culture using the same assumptions used during the Civil Rights and Black Consciousness generations, but the culture has shifted. African American congregations are trying to be invitational in the same ways they have always been in the past, but the culture has shifted. African American congregations are trying to ignite a flame in individuals in the same way they did during the Civil Rights and Black Consciousness generations, but the culture has shifted. It is time for African American congregations to rethink their assumptions and to reconnect to the shifting culture.

This means African American congregations have to become missional in new ways that speak to a shifting culture. It is no longer acceptable for congregations to expect the culture to conform to them. African American congregations have to start being more externally focused and reaching out to the culture. The dreams of the Civil Rights and Black Consciousness generations cannot be fully realized if congregations stop being innovative and fall into the very trap they fought against.

ASSUMPTIONS

Obviously it is impossible to name every assumption from the Civil Rights and Black Consciousness generations informing African American church life today. Let me highlight three (epicenter, shaped reality, and vision) that were instrumental in developing one of the most influential institutions in America. In today's shifting culture, however, these three assumptions are promoting an old-wineskin mentality in many African American congregations, creating unnecessary stumbling blocks.

EPICENTER

During the Civil Rights and Black Consciousness generations African American congregations were often the epicenter of the community. Many of the meetings were held in churches, rallies were held in churches, and churches were the base of operation for local activities. It did not matter whether one was churched or unchurched, there was a connection to a congregation.

In the Old Testament the temple is often described as being the epicenter of the Israelite community (Isaiah 2:1-3). The temple is portrayed as standing out above everything else in the community. It was the space in the community where individuals came expecting a sanctuary and to be given instruction for daily living. Many African American congregations during the Civil Rights and Black Consciousness generations fit the role that the temple played in Israelite daily living. These congregations stood out in the community and in many instances defined the community.

There are many reasons why African American congregations were the epicenter in the community. First, a more cohesive African American community existed during the Civil Rights and Black Consciousness generations. Most of the community lived on the same side of the tracks, regardless of one's economic status. I am not suggesting there were no divisions within the African American community, but that the community was together in one place. Many African American congregations were community congregations because the church anchored the community.

Second, the church was the most important institution within the community. The church was a space where African Americans were in control of their own reality. The church was a sanctuary in the truest sense of the word from the grind of life that many African Americans dealt with daily. It was the church that created an alternative reality to the harsh world on the other side of the doors, enabling many African Americans to have one space where they felt whole.

Third, for most African American denominations the church was the place where leaders were raised up (male leaders explicitly) to carry forward the mantle of justice. Individuals like Martin Luther King, Jr., Ralph Abernathy, and Jesse Jackson are just a few such leaders. Because the church was the epicenter in the community its leaders were often the central figures in the community. The expectation in many congregations was for the preacher to provide an intersection between religion, politics, and culture in a way that deepened one's spirituality while challenging the status quo.

African American churches were the epicenter in the community because they were communal congregations, they were the most important institution in the community, and many of the community leaders came out of them. Specifically for evangelism, this meant that African American congregations were not involved in evangelism or church growth *programs* because those happened naturally. African American churches were the most visible institution in the community and often provided the connecting glue.

Individuals wanted to share with others what was going on at the church. This was because many congregations were impacting the community and making a difference in the lives of people. Evangelism was not a special event, it was just practiced as a part of one's daily living. The ability to impact the community and embody the gospel in a way that provided an intersection between religion, politics, and culture helped to solidify African American congregations as the epicenter in the community.

But it is now the twenty-first century and many African American congregations are standing at the crossroads trying to hold on to that day when black churches were the epicenter of the community. Certainly not every congregation has ceased to be influential in African American communities, but the truth is most have lost their influence. Many African American congregations are virtually invisible in the community. These congregations are no longer impacting the community and often cannot name their neighbors.

The old-wineskin mentality that "People in the neighborhood will come because we are here" is no longer viable. This assumes the people in the community are still looking to the church for leadership. Things have shifted! Many in the post–civil rights generations are not even going to church. In many communities there are now community activists who have no official role in a faith community, but are better known than most preachers in the area.[4] These shifts are de-centering African American congregations from their place in the community.

Is your congregation experiencing a de-centering? The ability to articulate the shift that is occurring in our midst is important. African American congregations have to rethink what it means to be the church, not from a position of power, but from the perspective of being invisible. This is a tough pill to swallow. But congregations will just continue to stand at the crossroads or fall into the abyss if they do not make this shift.

SHAPED REALITY

Many people will remember the lyrics to Sam Cooke's famous song, "A Change Is Gonna Come." A part of the last stanza goes like this: "Oh there been times I thought I couldn't last for long / But I know a change gonna come, yes it will."[5] These words are representative of what many African American congregations stood for and lived out during the Civil Rights and Black Consciousness generations. African American congregations were able to shape the reality of the black community by inviting individuals to participate in the change that was coming. One of the fundamental contributions of African American congregations was convincing both blacks and whites that change was coming. African American congregations were able to shape reality in this way for two reasons.

First, African American congregations redefined black identity. There was a worldview created by some Anglos that African Americans were second-class citizens. In the South, but also in some places in the North, there were separate drinking fountains for African Americans and blacks were expected to sit at the back of the bus. African Americans were often the last hired and the first fired. Thus society sought to define the personhood of African Americans in a particular manner.

African American congregations shaped a different identity for blacks. They constructed an identity that valued individuals and treated them as first-class citizens. Following the example of Jesus, many African American congregations invited individuals to see themselves differently in relation to the world. For example, Jesus invited the woman from Samaria (John 4:1-42) to perceive herself not as a second-class person, but as one worthy of a religious dialogue with a male. Jesus valued her as an individual even though she was female and from Samaria (Jews and Samaritans did not get along). Jesus not only took the initiative to talk to her, but sent her to tell others about the conversation. This indicates that Jesus trusted her to be an ambassador and was not concerned about how society defined her status.

African American congregations invited those inside and outside of the church to perceive themselves differently. Congregations did this by emphasizing that everyone is made in the image of God and should be treated as a child of God. This attitude became so deeply embedded within African American culture that it became one of the main themes of the Black Consciousness generation. The culmination of this new identity was James Brown's "Say it Loud, I'm Black and I'm Proud!" The point was not to pit blacks against whites, but to value African Americans as being fully human.

African American congregations identifying themselves as fully human set an expectation for how others should identify and treat them. African American congregations were redefining history in a way that promoted their inclusion in society. The expectation of the Samaritan woman was that Jesus would treat her like others and make her invisible. The fact that Jesus saw her and included her in God's mission redefined her understanding of herself. This is what African American congregations did for many blacks: the church redefined their understanding of self by not allowing others to define who they were.

Second, African American congregations shaped reality by being counter-cultural. The term *counter-cultural* is bandied about by many individuals. The suggestion is the church needs to be counter-cultural. A common question is, "What does this look like in practice?" One of the strengths of African American congregations during the Civil Rights era was how they embodied what it meant to be counter-cultural by proclamation and deeds.

Preachers and laity spoke out against the injustices facing African Americans. This was done in the church and outside of the church. The quintessential example is Martin Luther King Jr., who used biblical imagery in his speeches both inside and outside of the church.[6] It was not simply using biblical images that made King and others remarkable speakers, but the ability to connect those images to the lives of everyday people. Think about it! The power of King's "Letter from a Birmingham Jail" was that it painted a different picture of reality than most African Americans readily understood and were testifying to all over the United States.

African Americans were testifying to a reality where they were included in the phrase "American citizen." These testimonies challenged the status quo. It was African American congregations that prepared people to testify against the status quo. The testimonies not only challenged the status quo, the testimonies invited others to come and participate in shaping a different reality. This invitation was not coerced, but naturally flowed from individuals who believed they were following Jesus. Jesus invited the disciples to come and participate in kingdom building. There was no coercion or promise of riches, simply an invitation to participate in God's mission for the world. African American congregations believed they were participating in God's mission for the world.

Most African American congregations did not simply proclaim a different reality was possible, but they also did deeds to shape or make that reality possible. They protested against the old reality through marches, sit-ins, and other activities. It is one thing to proclaim "I want to be treated as a full human being"; it is another to go sit at a lunch counter where you are not welcome, living out that proclamation. The latter is an enactment of a different reality from the one that currently exists.

African American congregations prepared individuals to enact a different reality. Most of the congregations supported individuals who were participating by bailing them out of jail, feeding them and their families, and making sure they were trained. So the invitation to participate in God's mission was not a calling to a few, but the entire congregation had a role it could play. Some were out visibly protesting, while others were in the background, but still instrumental to the protest movement.

One way to name what was happening in congregations is the phrase "persuasive witness." African American congregations were a persuasive witness to a culture where all was not right in Zion and some things needed to change. The witnessing was done in both word and deed in a manner that shaped reality to conform toward what many believed to be the kingdom of God. The ability of African American congregations to continally invite others to participate speaks to how persuasive many churches were in shaping a counter-cultural reality.

But it is the twenty-first century, and many African American congregations are still standing at the crossroads trying to hold on to that day when African American congregations were persuasive witnesses. These congregations have bought into an old-wineskin mentality that needs examining. **How are congregations currently defining God's mission? Who are congregations now inviting to participate in God's mission?** It was clear (for the most part) during the Civil Rights and Black Consciousness generations what the mission of the church was in society. African American congregations were able to shape the reality of the community around this mission.

Evangelism was not about filling pews or giving money to maintain structures. Evangelism focused on inviting individuals to participate in changing society and the world. Some congregations will take offence and argue, "We are still missional focused. We feed the hungry and provide services for those in need." This is true. The challenge, however, is in valuing the identity of those being helped and not marginalizing them.

A part of standing at the crossroads for many congregations involves facing an internal crisis between those handing out goods and those receiving the handouts. Too many congregations have a class divide where those handing out goods perceive themselves to be doing a favor to those receiving the handouts. The divide is not only economic but generational. In many African American congregations the leadership still resembles a

Civil Rights and Black Consciousness style. The evangelism these congregations do also resembles that style.

Evangelism is not about developing a certain type of model, but it is about allowing everyone's gift to enhance the kingdom. I know it is hard for some to imagine, but the reality is Dr. King would have a hard time being a leader in many congregations today. Many African American congregations have shaped reality in such a way that only those who were a part of the Civil Rights or Black Consciousness generations can be in leadership. Those in the post–civil rights generations are excluded. One of the strengths of the Civil Rights movement was that it was intergenerational and one of its primary leaders (King) was under forty. Now the church is no longer intergenerational and congregations are trying to figure out how to attract younger people. **Does this sound like your congregation?**

The ability of African American congregations to shape reality is diminishing because congregations are struggling to define what it means to participate in God's mission. They are struggling because marginalized individuals[7] and many in the post–civil rights generations do not feel valued by congregations. This is a huge shift from the Civil Rights and Black Consciousness generations. It is a shift that has to be addressed if congregations are going to be missional again. It is a shift that requires congregations to be invitational in new ways to those in the post–civil rights generations.

VISION

Habakkuk 2:2 reads, "Then the LORD answered me and said, / Write a vision, / and make it plain upon a tablet / so that a runner can read it." The Civil Rights and Black Consciousness generations wrote the vision and made it plain. It was not a vision of their own making, but a vision grounded in God's mission. The vision was a new society where African Americans and Anglo Americans not only could co-exist but were in community together. African American congregations contributed to this re-visioning of society in three ways.

NEW PICTURE

There are many reasons King's "I Have a Dream" speech is remembered as one of the best of all time. For our purposes it is one of the best because it developed a vision for society, rooted in the biblical ideal of a new day. The Isaiah 11:6 text that talks about opposites being able to live together in a new way was the picture King painted in this speech. King's point was that although this vision is not a reality now, as a country we are moving toward this reality. Like an artist who gives everyone a paint brush, King sketched a picture of the future and invited others to add their strokes to the canvas.

Certainly King was a clarion voice in sketching out the vision, but it was not just his vision. African American congregations were active not only in being the canvas, but in providing the brushes and colors. Many African American congregations were the canvas for the vision by the way they allowed the public as a whole to be voyeurs in their midst. These congregations ignited for those inside and outside of the church a desire for something new. In biblical language, these congregations gave the world a glimpse of the kingdom of God.

In Matthew, Mark, and Luke, Jesus makes numerous references to the kingdom of God. This was the vision that Jesus set before the people. This is the challenge that the Civil Rights generation set before the people while trying to fully grasp what it meant to participate in such a grand vision. The vision of a society where blacks and whites dine together and walk hand in hand was a grand dream. It was a dream rooted in the belief that the Spirit ignites in all of us a desire for community—not an exclusive community, but an inclusive community that mirrors the radical vision of supposed opposites coming together in a different way.

The power of a vision is that it gives people something to believe in and work toward. African American congregations understood that the challenge before them was to help others see and work for the same vision. But work is more than simply doing a task. In this instance, work meant the willingness to follow a spiritual discipline, even when some perceived it as counter to their lived reality. Practices like prayer, non-violence, singing, and testifying were all disciplines that pointed to a new vision for society. It was these practices that made the vision plain—that made it possible for insiders and outsiders to join in and feel like they were a part of something grand, yet not so grand as to be improbable.

AWARENESS

During the time of the Civil Rights movement many Americans wondered why a different society was necessary. If you were African American it probably was obvious, but this was not the case for everyone. The oppressive structure of society were invisible to some because it did not impede their progress. African American congregations had to create an awareness of the challenges blacks faced because of the structures of society. Think about Jesus talking with the Samaritan woman, trying to explain to her the deeper meaning of living water. Her understanding of water was shaped by going to get water at the well, so until Jesus made her aware of a different type of water it made no sense.

The need for a different vision often makes no sense to those who have constructed their lives around the old vision. For example, the 1967 movie *Guess Who's Coming to Dinner* helped people to construct a different reality. Katherine Hepburn invited an African American male (Sidney Poitier) to dinner to meet her family, and this caused a rupture to their old worldview. Spencer Tracy, who played the father, had to start constructing a new vision of society where Anglos and African Americans dated one another. The movie was a window for others to start constructing a new vision of society.

African American congregations helped those inside and outside of the church develop a different awareness of the current conditions and therefore the need for a different vision. One example of this was the Montgomery bus boycott. African American congregations wanted to make the bus company and others aware of the injustice of blacks having to sit at the back of the bus or give up their seat for an Anglo person. Rosa Parks set things in motion when she refused to give up her seat on the bus.

The boycott was not only an effective economic strategy against the bus company, it was also effective at raising awareness in the country of how this practice did not fit with a biblical vision of living and flourishing together. Developing an awareness of a new vision often means helping individuals to let go of ideas they have held for ages. It was African American congregations that pricked the conscience of America on the one side, while holding up a different vision of how to move forward on the other side.

African American congregations made people aware that a new reality was possible by getting their attention and pointing them in a different direction. This is part of the mastery of Maya Angelou's poem "I Know Why the Caged Bird Sings." This poem contrasts the reality of never being able to flourish with the possibility of flourishing when given an opportunity. African American congregations understood this tension and made those who did not face this reality aware of this tension.

PARTICIPATION

One of the great achievements of the Civil Rights and Black Consciousness generations was igniting a flame in those outside of the community to participate in constructing a new society. African American congregations welcomed the participation of all in standing up for justice. The vision was not for a society constructed by and for African Americans, but for a society that was inclusive of all people. This meant involving those not a part of the community in the work of justice.

A few outsiders who played a role in the fight for freedom were Abraham Joshua Heschel and Branch Rickey. Heschel was a Jewish rabbi who bought into the vision and worked to bring it to fruition. Rickey signed Jackie Robinson as the first African American to get a major league baseball contract. Heschel, Rickey, and others like them could have chosen to stay quiet and not disrupt the apple cart. While they might have agreed in principle with African American congregations on the need for a new vision, putting their lives on the line required a different level of commitment. Heschel, Rickey, and others outside of the African American community were willing to move away from the norm toward a reality that many thought was improbable. In many cases, the work of African American congregations directly or indirectly ignited the flame that made participating in a new vision something all segments of society perceived as necessary.

For example, in 1967 Carl Stokes became the first African American to become the mayor of a major city—Cleveland, Ohio. The vision of a new reality ignited people to think differently in all aspects of their life, including politics. Without input and participation from those outside of the African American community, a new reality would not have been possible. The vision created by African American congregations captivated people in such a way that they were ready to let go of old ideas and to move forward in a different way.

It is the twenty-first century and many African American congregations are standing at the crossroads trying to hold on to that vision. It's a vision that without question has been instrumental in transforming society, but a vision that no longer captivates the imagination of the post–civil rights generations or the wider public. **What parts of the Civil Rights and Black Consciousness generations' vision is your congregation holding on to?**

The pendulum has swung in the other direction and African American congregations have to take notice. It was hard for many Anglos to let go of old ideas and to buy into a new vision. Now it is time for many African American congregations to let go of older ideas and to buy into a new vision.

The power of the Civil Rights and Black Consciousness vision ignited a desire for people to be educated differently, which is a part of discipleship. African American congregations did not go out and seek people to disciple. The people came to them seeking to be disciples. The people came because they believed in the vision. The vision made sense as a way of moving forward.

One can argue about whether the vision has ever been fully realized. It is true that society changed and some integration did occur. The Integrationist generation is the bridge between the Civil Rights era and those who have only read about civil rights in a book. Some in this generation are old enough to appreciate the struggle and the old-wineskin mentality. Even for some in the Integrationist generation the vision is no longer captivating. The result is that many African American congregations are declining and are having a hard time connecting to those who do not buy into the old ideas.

A missional congregation understands that while the idea of the kingdom of God is eternal, the way that vision gets expressed and lived out will change. This is not a denial of what has come previously, but a recognition of the way in which people and society are always in flux. The ability to reconstruct the vision to speak to the new reality is critical. It is what missional congregations have to do!

CROSSROADS

This chapter describes some of the assumptions undergirding the Civil Rights and Black Consciousness generations and the power of these assumptions for today's black congregations. I believe it is time to reinterpret these assumptions from a post–civil rights perspective. The old assumptions created an old-wineskin mentality that is pervasive in African American church culture. This is not an "old versus new" argument. My point is that it is no longer feasible to assume a shared worldview between the church and community that allows the church to maintain its old understandings. The truth is, African American congregations unwilling to engage the cultural shift or to admit that we are at a crossroads will eventually become irrelevant.

Some individuals will remember African American insurance companies that sold burial policies. At one point in African American history these companies were essential and provided the only way for many African Americans to get insurance. As the culture shifted many of these companies were absorbed or changed with the shifting culture. They still were in the insurance business, but they offered products more connected to the times. The African American church is going to have to do the same as we move forward into a new century. The next chapter will explore ways African American congregations can reclaim their innovative edge.

REVISITING THE QUESTIONS

1. How are congregations going to move forward? Do we want to remain standing at the crossroads? (page 26)

2. Is your congregation experiencing a de-centering? Do you feel like the floor is falling from underneath you? (page 31)

3. How are congregations currently defining God's mission? How is your congregation making a difference in your community? (page 35)

4. Does this sound like your congregation? Are you consistently saying you need more young people in the congregation? (page 36)

5. What parts of the Civil Rights and Black Consciousness generations' vision is your congregation holding on to? What are you willing to let go of to move forward? (page 41)

ACTIVITIES

1. Read Luke 24:13-35—Think about the assumptions the travelers were holding on to regarding Jesus' death.

2. Make a list of the assumptions and practices you are perpetuating from the 1950s and 60s. Consider those things you can rethink or do away with altogether.

CHAPTER 3
NEW WINESKINS

Prayin' for all of those who ain't got it . . .
Yeah, the people starvin' for something new, we starving for it.[1]

K weli claims the "people are starvin' for something new," and although he is describing a particular situation facing many in the ghetto, his words are also prophetic towards many African American congregations—"people are starving for something new," a new way of thinking about church that connects African Americans with those of the post–civil rights generations. If African American churches are going to be missional, then rethinking a Civil Rights theological perspective is necessary.

This does not require throwing the baby out with the bath water! It does require, however, reinterpreting certain assumptions toward a more missional and inclusive understanding of what it means to be a congregation. To this end, congregations must resist remaining comfortable in ways that maintain the status quo and lead to congregational decline.[2] Missional congregations avoid decline by embodying the gospel story in a way that maintains the integrity of the gospel, while recognizing that no one person or group controls the gospel. If it is true that no one person or group controls the gospel, then collaborating with others on the embodiment of the gospel involves the broader community and not just a select few. By broadening their embodiment of the gospel, congregations will empower individuals in a way that is invitational and not an "us versus them" mentality. This chapter develops an ecclesiology that is inclusive of the voices of the post–civil rights generations by rethinking concepts like space, collaboration, and empowerment.

SPACE

The importance of space should not be underestimated for post–civil rights generations. Space is personal and communal. Space is physical and spiritual. Space is physical in the way we claim certain territories or areas, and spiritual because one is always trying to move toward being in a good space (or place) in life. The ability to carve out one's own space is important and a part of an on-going spiritual journey, but it is also important to find one's space in a community. Those of us in the church often believe only churchgoers are on a spiritual journey. The truth is everyone is trying to make sense out of their lives at some level and seeking both private and communal space to make this happen. Unfortunately many individuals in the post–civil rights generations are finding ways outside of the church to create those places of sanctuary. The way those who are a part of the post–civil rights generations negotiate these understandings of space often are counter-intuitive to earlier African American generations.

Lauryn Hill expresses the sentiment of many in the post–civil rights generations when she says, "All these traditions killin' freedom, Is the reason I must change."[3] While her words are not directed toward the African American church, it is not a stretch to interpret them in the light of the post-civil rights generations' dissatisfaction with institutional religion. The dissatisfaction often centers on a feeling of being boxed into a certain way of believing and doing that is not open to questioning. Hill is challenging this mindset by claiming that those beholden to doing things in particular ways cannot define another's reality.

The problem is that the Civil Rights generation wants to define the meaning of space for post–civil rights generations. One can interpret Hill's lyrics as suggesting the institutional church is mistaken if it thinks it can define reality for those in the post–civil rights era simply because it is the church. She correctly points out that those in the post–civil rights generations "can't be chained." They have either gotten out or stayed away from many African American congregations. Many congregations are waiting on those in the post–civil rights generations to change and to become comfortable in their space, but have been reluctant to hear the voices of the post–civil rights generations.

Let me quickly squash any notions that I am suggesting that congregations give up the heart of the gospel message to become relevant to those who are staying away. While the Christian narrative is not monolithic, the heart of the narrative is Christ-centered and this pattern cannot be dismissed just for the sake of getting people in pews. I do believe, however, that congregations can alter the way they live out the gospel story and listen to the voices of others who are engaging the story in authentic and creative ways. The distinction is about promoting certain ways of thinking institutionally instead of a willingness to make space for new voices in the community to live out the narrative. The question is, **"How can African American congregations make space so that the voices of all generations can be heard?"**

While various answers are possible to the question of making space, a good way forward comes from the Gospels. The

Gospels of Matthew (1:1-16) and Luke (3:23-38) give a genealogy for Jesus, but the genealogies look different. The Gospel of Luke only names men and traces Jesus' genealogy back to Adam. The Gospel of Matthew names men and women, some of whom have interesting stories. Ruth is a foreigner who marries into the Israelite family, but space is made for her. The wife of Uriah (Bathsheba) becomes David's wife after he has her husband killed. The point is Matthew does not give us a sterile genealogy, but includes the dysfunction that permeates Jesus' heritage. He sets up Jesus' birth to Mary by implying that God throughout history makes space for those who don't quite fit our paradigms.

The expectation was that the Messiah should have a strong bloodline and be born into a royal family. God disrupts our expectations in the Matthew genealogy and birth narrative by highlighting those who are outside of the norm. Jesus' bloodline includes foreigners and Jesus' mother is a pregnant teenager. If God makes space for non-traditional ways of conceiving, then are congregations called to do any less? This is one of the challenges facing African American congregations as they attempt to live out and into the mission of God today.

Trying to connect with the post–civil rights generations poses a challenge because the Civil Rights and Black Consciousness generations are having difficulty making space. The post–civil rights generations seek to connect spiritually with God, others, and themselves. They are looking for spaces where they can make these connections. The idea of sanctuary is not necessarily the church building where everyone used to come and gather, but it is a space that allows for a certain connection that is not easily defined. Unlike many in earlier African American generations, younger people are often willing to seek this space outside of the institutional church.

DEFINING ONE'S SPACE

This means institutional churches have to rethink their understanding of sanctuary in the following ways. First, the ability to define one's space for oneself is essential. The post–civil rights generations do not want the meaning of sanctuary defined for them. They want to discover for themselves what it means to be in relationship to the Holy and how the Holy is in relationship to them. KRS-One, an old-school, socially conscious rapper, pushes the Christian envelope in a rap entitled "The Truth." He raps, "You gotta look within yourself, not a scripture. KRS-One comes to rearrange the God picture."[4] One way to interpret these lines and the entirety of the rap is to perceive them as confrontational toward the Bible and ultimately God. Another way to understand them is as the story of people on a spiritual journey, like we are as Christians, and trying to make sense of life.

The tendency is for many African American congregations to choose the former interpretation and to denigrate the insights of those seeking a deeper understanding of God. This process of being denigrated and told you don't understand God, the Bible, and life leads to distancing oneself from those making these claims. It pushes those being denigrated to look within themselves for answers and a place of sanctuary that is not open to those in congregations. This solution is not a rejection of God but is a rejection of institutional religion.

It is also problematic for some when neo-soul artists like Jill Scott seek to create a space where they can connect with God by using resources other than the Bible. On her hit single "A Long

Walk" from her first album, Scott references the Koran and the Bible as natural ways to engage in dialogue about the realities of life.[5] Her point is that she is willing to use all resources available to her to figure things out and to create a good space for herself. This approach is in direct conflict with many African American congregations that believe reading any other source besides the Bible is blasphemous.

Josef Sorett discusses this eclecticism in an article for *religion dispatches* about the leader of the Wu Tang Clan RZA (Robert Diggs). He writes:

> Ultimately, it is the apparent earnestness of RZA's spiritual quest that is most interesting in *The Tao of Wu*, even as one may question the ethics of many of his actions. One is made witness to his efforts to make sense of the messiness (and meaning) of his life, of black life in the United States, and of *life*, more generally—both as memories and in real time. As RZA dines at the postmodern buffet of American religion, the delicacies include ample portions of Christian Bible (with a preference for wisdom literature and John's Gospel) and Eastern religion and philosophy (including citations of Lao Tzu, the Buddha, and Rumi), and a plethora of pop-culture references. . . . And while he seems to have pulled it all together seamlessly for himself, many will find only madness in his methods.[6]

Sorett points out the challenge facing many African American congregations to make space for post–civil rights generations who reject a singular view of faith and are often spiritually eclectic. They are not denying the importance of spirituality or even God, but they are making the church rethink the meaning of sacred space. Sacred space is not confined to doing things in a particular way in a particular building, but has to do with the way we live and interact in all parts of our lives. Many in the post–civil rights generations are willing to pull from or combine all spiritual resources that will help them get to that space. This scares many people in congregations who perceive it as an attack against God and them. Maybe it is time for those in congregations to perceive it as an openness to going on a journey and not a personal attack against their faith.

It is dangerous to make generalizations, but I think it is fair to suggest that those in post–civil rights generations are open to exploring how to be connected to God. Many institutional churches, however, have failed to maintain a healthy dialogue with these generations as they think about dealing with life's realities and their relationship to God. Many African American congregations are only willing to engage in a comfortable dialogue that asks certain types of questions that fit into a pre-conceived mold. Missional congregations have to be open to helping those outside of the institutional church to explore connections as they seek to find safe spaces in their lives.

This means redefining sanctuary as a sacred space where God is present, but not necessarily confined to a particular physical space. It means helping individuals to connect the ways in which their personal journey is a part of the communal journey toward wholeness. It means being open to the reality that folk will bring questions about other faith traditions than Christianity. The question is, **"Is your congregation willing to create a space for those who are truly seeking a relationship with God?"**

This is not new for African Americans. Our African American foreparents, many of whom were slaves in the United States, engaged Christianity from the perspective of their traditional African religions.[7] They understood that God did not reside in one particular place, but was in the midst of their community whether it was in Africa or America. The focus was not on a particular place or way to worship God. The focus was on worshiping God in a manner that helped them to make sense out of their lived reality. Reclaiming this ideal of sanctuary not as one place or a way of worshiping means congregations have to rethink the way they create spaces in the worshiping community for those who are not insiders.

Congregations are called to embody the gospel not in a particular way, but in a manner that allows for individuals to experience the working of the Holy Spirit. It requires developing a different mindset that focuses on helping people to experience God where they are and not where the church building is located. It means post–civil rights generations will not be expected to conform to the congregation's understanding of space just because it has always been done that way! It means that congregations are willing to share the gospel in ways and spaces where they may be uncomfortable.

A REAL COMMUNITY

Second, the post–civil rights generations seek "real" community. By "real," I mean a community where people are not pretending or promoting something false. Whether we like it or not, because of the class divide within the African American community, the institutional church, at times, does not keep it real. We drive to church and ignore the neighborhood where the church resides and drive out again a couple of hours later. Tupac Shakur recorded a rap titled, "I Wonder If Heaven Got a

Ghetto?" Shakur is pushing the question of keeping it real even in the next world. One can interpret him as rapping to God and saying, "If I make it to heaven, then I want to be with those who were real with me down here on earth and were not phony."

We may disagree with Shakur's theology and argue he was the epitome of someone outside of the Christian faith, but he pushes us to rethink how we are missional in the church. If those outside of the church are not interested in being in community with us in the afterlife, then what message are we sending to them in this life? Creating a space that is welcoming to those outside of our comfort zones means dealing with the tough realities of life. Shakur is clear that one way or another, those interested in keeping it real will find a space to do so—even in heaven.

Keeping it real means talking with those in the community about issues they confront and not talking about them. The former implies a dialogue, the latter a monologue. Congregations have to be willing to be a space where dialogues can occur and not just monologues. A dialogue means both sides have something to offer and a willingness to listen. A communal space is a place where everyone feels at home and not just a few people. Missional congregations have to create an environment where individuals feel at home because they are connected to a community that is keeping it real.

Space is personal and communal. Space is physical and spiritual. Becoming a missional congregation means altering one's perception of space in a way that challenges assumptions that maintain the comfort of the institution. It means a willingness to create an environment where others can come and feel safe. It means going out and being uncomfortable in other spaces. In terms of evangelism this requires listening and hearing the challenge of the gospel in a new way from voices that are outside of one's comfort zone. It is a space where people can keep it real and feel free to talk about God without being denigrated.

SEEN AND HEARD

Many of us have heard the saying, "Children are to be seen, but not heard." There are many issues with this statement. One of them is that congregations are applying this statement not only to younger folk, but to outsiders. The idea behind this statement is one day your time will come, but until that day be satisfied to be seen. When is that day? Congregations have to become more collaborative in working with those, inside and outside of the church, who have no real voice. Whether you are younger and never have any "real" input into the lived faith of the congregation or an outsider not really welcome in the faith community, a congregation that is more collaborative is a welcome change from the status quo.

Many of us forget that Jesus, according to Luke 3:23, was in the thirty-something age bracket. Jesus also was not from the "right" family. Jesus, like many younger people today and/or people not blessed to live in certain places, was not always warmly welcomed by the elders in the community. They ran Jesus out of town (Luke 4:28-30), they questioned his practices (Luke 5:33-34), and they even disapproved of his willingness to forgive others (Luke 5:21-22). Jesus was not a part of the insiders because he brought new ideas and ways of doing things to the table.

It is one thing to read the Gospels and side with Jesus as an insider in the church—which we all do. It is really eye-opening to read the Gospel and to think of Jesus as an outsider and those of us in institutional churches as the insiders opposing new ideas and practices. Think about how difficult it was for the Pharisees and scribes to embrace Jesus. Is this any different from us embracing those in the post–civil rights generations coming with new ideas and practices? Is this any different from us embracing those in the community where the church resides who do not live in our neighborhood? We often interpret these questions in a way that makes Jesus a part of the religious establishment and point out that we are talking about individuals who are truly outside of the church.

This line of reasoning is not helpful for institutional churches, because it ignores the fact that, while Jesus was a part of the Jewish tradition, Jesus never bought into the practice of making certain individuals invisible in the community. Jesus did not promote a mentality of "I am blessed and you are not." In Luke 13:10-17, Jesus heals a woman who is crippled on the Sabbath day. The leader of the synagogue is a witness to this healing and admonishes Jesus for healing on the Sabbath and not on another day. Typically we read this text and cheer Jesus for standing up to the leader in the synagogue. We (in many institutional churches) usually do not read this text and consider that we are the leaders in the synagogue admonishing those who seek to do new things even when they are not opposed to the gospel.

My point is that Jesus did not settle for being seen and not heard. Jesus did not want others like the crippled woman to be invisible either. Jesus lived and proclaimed a gospel that was both challenging and a blessing for everyone. The gospel was not just about a few being blessed at the expense of others. A part of the challenge of the gospel is setting a table where all are welcome and have a voice. This requires authentic invitation and authentic hospitality.

Jesus realized that the religious establishment during his day was not always willing to extend authentic invitation and hospitality. Therefore, Jesus called twelve disciples who were willing to interpret God's calling on their lives differently from others and especially those in the establishment. These twelve were to be the start of a community that challenged not only cultural practices, but the institutional practices of the day. They were called to work collaboratively as a community to point people to a new way of existing.

Becoming a missional church requires rethinking the belief that outsiders and some insiders should be seen and not heard. It means reinventing one's congregation to become a place where everyone has a voice and not just a few. On his 1999 CD *Nastradamus*, Nas drops these words: "He who has ears, let him hear and he who has sight, let him see / Those who know don't talk and those who talk don't know a thing."[8] These lyrics are a challenge to many congregations to start seeing and hearing the voices of those not included in the dialogue. This requires a shift from privileging a few to seeking the insights of various voices. Doing this will impact congregations in the following ways.

First, it will redefine relationships inside of the church toward becoming more collaborative. This means congregations will be more intentional in developing a leadership style that includes the voices of all generations. Certainly this assumes a congregation has multiple generations. If it does, then taking the insights of those in the post–civil rights generations seriously is critical— and not just on "special days"! The voices of all generations will be heard in determining the shape of worship, finances, and all other activities of the congregation.

The Civil Rights generation protested against discriminatory practices that did not give them a voice in the process. For example, laws that deterred African Americans from voting were challenged. The goal was not to destroy the process but to be an active part of the process. By analogy, post–civil rights generations want to be a part of the process in congregations. They are not trying to destroy the congregation, but want their voices heard. Congregations have to be willing to hear their voices or be boycotted.

Second, it will redefine relationships with those outside of the church toward becoming more collaborative. This is where the rubber hits the road because this is where many of our congregations struggle. They do not perceive the need to be collaborative with those outside of the congregation. This form of collaboration requires listening to why those on the outside do not perceive the congregation as a viable place for their spiritual journey. It does not mean promoting some watered-down version of the gospel.

One of the fascinating themes in the gospel is that often after Jesus heals someone he sends them to the temple and priest (for example, Mark 1:40-44). These individuals were excluded from temple life before the healing because of their condition. If someone was physically imperfect, then they were not allowed to go into the temple. One can interpret Jesus as sending a message that those in the temple were missing the point by ignoring those outside of the temple who were disconnected from the community. The powers that be were ignoring those who had no voice because they believed they had nothing to add to the communal life. They were not blessed!

Many congregations are operating the same way as those in the temple and ignoring those on the outside because they believe they have nothing to add to the life of the congregation. One of the realities of the gospel is that the congregation is called to engage these individuals in a way that may reshape congregational life. By collaborating with those on the outside a congregation can begin to hear how it really needs to change its hospitality and the way it integrates folk into the life of the believing community. The perspective they bring is not the same old way of doing business, but the perspective of those who have been ignored for whatever reason.

Stevie Wonder is one of the giants in R&B and came into prominence during the late sixties. Stevie Wonder collaborated with Busta Rhymes on a song called "Been Through the Storm." Stevie Wonder has every right to be picky about whom he collaborates with musically, and Busta Rhymes is not the first person that may come to mind to work with Stevie Wonder. Stevie Wonder has done many such collaborations over the years. Congregations can learn from these collaborations that it is possible for different generations to work together and for those who are revered insiders to work with those outside of their genre. It pushes both sides to learn and expand their understanding of reality.

Becoming a missional congregation means learning and expanding one's understanding of reality in the midst of sharing the gospel. Missional congregations are willing to open themselves up to outsiders because they are not afraid of change. They do not change for the sake of change, but they are willing to be in conversation with the voiceless. Turn the tables and think about becoming a part of a community where you have no voice.

Congregations need to ask, **"Why would I attend or become a part of a community where I am not valued?"** Congregations are called to think about this question and to answer honestly. Think about it! Are we a place where people are seen and heard? Are we a place that perpetuates an insider (Pharisees) mentality? Missional congregations are always looking for opportunities for collaboration with others that allow for more than one voice to be heard.

SPIRITUAL EMPOWERMENT

One of the challenges in life is getting exactly what we are seeking. If I go to church with a mindset that the worship experience is going to be boring, then it is often boring. If I go with the mindset that it will be off the chain because a certain choir is singing, guess what? It is usually off the chain and I will declare that the Spirit was really moving in the service. My point is, consciously or unconsciously, often our attitude predetermines our openness to the movement of the Spirit. This can cause an "us versus them" mentality depending on how you hope the Spirit will move.

Reclaiming a biblical focus on spiritual empowerment can move us beyond these splits toward a more holistic embodiment of our faith. In the Gospel of John (14:16-17), Jesus prepares the disciples for the coming of the Holy Spirit. The Gospel of John uses the Greek word *paraclete*, which often gets translated as Advocate (John 14:16, NRSV), to describe the Holy Spirit. Jesus is telling the disciples that when he disappears an advocate will come that will teach them and remind them of Jesus' teachings (John 14:26). Another way to think about it is the Holy Spirit comes to stand with us and gives us insights and knowledge for living out our Christian faith. The Holy Spirit empowers us for seeing, understanding, and living that continues the work of Jesus.

Following this logic it means we have to be careful about the way we describe the Spirit moving in a congregation. Congregations should not simply equate high emotional services with the movement of the Spirit. I am not suggesting that the Spirit is not moving in these services, but we fool ourselves if we think emotion easily translates into the movement of the Spirit. In Luke 4:18-19 when Jesus says the Spirit has come upon him, he describes how the Spirit is empowering him to create a different reality for the downtrodden. The Spirit gives Jesus the eyes to see the world differently and to understand the ways in which the world is counter to the pattern of God's reign.

Congregations have to open themselves up to the Spirit moving in ways they never imagined. No one person or congregation controls the Spirit or the workings of the Spirit. If the Spirit is calling congregations to see the world differently and to understand the ways in which the world is counter to the pattern of God's reign, then congregations need to be discerning. I believe a part of this discernment is seeing through the eyes of someone like Tupac, who challenges us in "Hail Mary" to really see reality for those living in some urban cores. The chorus is, "Come with me, Hail Mary; Run quick see, what do we have here."[9]

Tupac is using a Catholic understanding of Hail Mary (the greeting by Gabriel to Mary—"Greetings, blessed one") to challenge those in congregations to come and see what is really happening in the community. Tupac puts a different twist on the greeting by challenging the blessed ones in congregations to get out of their comfort zones and experience reality in the community. Tupac's question is, "How can you tell me how to live if you have no under-standing of my circumstances?" To be spiritually empowered means the ability to discern how the Spirit is working inside of us and out-side of the congregation. We do the Spirit an injustice when we bottle it up in a way that keeps it inside of the church. Missional congregations are called to reclaim a more holisitic understanding of the Spirit that opens them up to new possibilities because they see, think, and live differently.

In terms of the post–civil rights generations, one of these pos-sibilities is a new way of communicating. It is easy to read Acts 2 and get caught up in the excitement of the Spirit descending "like a tongue" on those in the Upper Room, prompting observers to think they are drunk. One can just picture how amazing this scene must have been and the energy in that place.

But we should not miss that while the Spirit worked on the inside of individuals, the Spirit also manifested itself in breaking down language barriers. In Acts 2:6 it reads, "And at this sound the crowd gathered and was bewildered, because each one heard them speaking in the native language of each." The Spirit enabled them to understand those who spoke a different language and to hear them for the first time. While those in the post–civil rights generations are not speaking a foreign language in the technical sense, it sounds foreign to many in the Civil Rights and Black Consciousness generations.

There is a breakdown in communication that has to bridged. Talib Kweli says these words in a rap called "Listen":

> Ladies and gentlemen, get ready here it come {"Listen!"} . . .
> It's for your spirits so, but y'all don't hear me though
> {"Listen!"}[10]

Kweli is telling us to listen because he is about to say something important. What he is going to say is good for our spirits. The truth is congregations are struggling because the different generations do not really hear one another. There may be a lot of banging on the eardrum by both sides, but the words sound foreign. Although Kweli does not take the rap in this direction, I believe he is on the right track in claiming listening is good for our spirits. Not only is it good for our spirits, but it is the Spirit who will enable us to bridge the communication gap.

Becoming a missional congregation means a willingness to let the Spirit open your ears in a way that you can comprehend that which is foreign. Think about it! **How can you invite individuals to be a part of your community if you cannot communicate with them?** This does not mean congregations should simply start using street vernacular, because it will be inauthentic. It does mean opening one's self up to the Spirit so that communication is possible and you are able to hear and comprehend what is being said. Indie Arie on her *Testimony Vol. 1* project *Life and Relationships* has a tune called "Better People." Her refrain is if older generations and younger generations communicate with one another we all will become better people.[11] What we cannot accomplish on our own is possible if we follow the guidance of the Spirit. We can become better people.

Next, the Spirit empowers us to act boldly for others. We should be mindful that even when we experience a personal transformation by the Spirit, it's so we can act counter to the world's expectations. In Acts 25:25-30 we pick up the story of Paul and Silas in jail. The two of them, along with the other prisoners, are praying and singing and an earthquake breaks off their chains and opens the doors of the prison. If we were wrongly imprisoned and the doors of the prison opened, most of us would immediately get out. The jailer in the story had fallen asleep, and when he awakes and sees the doors of the prison open he believes that Paul and the others are gone. The expectation is that they would have taken advantage of the situation.

The jailer is surprised when Paul calls out from inside the prison that they are all still there. Paul and the others went counter to the expectation of the jailor and most of us. They acted boldly in this situation because they were empowered by the Spirit, even though it could result in their staying imprisoned. African American history is replete with examples of individuals being empowered by the Spirit to act boldly for others. Harriet Tubman, Sojourner Truth, and Martin Luther King, Jr., are just a few examples in African American history.

The idea of the Spirit empowering us to act boldly is nothing new. What is needed in many congregations is reclaiming a holistic understanding of the Spirit. The movement of the Spirit is not about differentiating something I/we have and others do not. The movement of the Spirit is about being transformed in a way that our gifts are used to create a different reality in the congregation and community. The Spirit is about transforming individuals toward a community that is a foretaste of the reign of God. This sounds like a pie-in-the-sky thought, but as Mos Def points out, "There Is a Way!"[12] Mos Def challenges us in this tune to believe "no one has to be left out" and "there is a way no matter what anyone may say."[13] The Spirit is about guiding us toward greater possibilities so that no one has to be left out.

Becoming a missional congregation means a willingness to be guided by the Spirit toward greater possibilities. It is a recognition that with the Spirit there is a way forward if we are willing to act boldly. These bold acts are for the benefit of community and not the destruction of community. Think about it: **How would your congregation be different if it acted boldly to construct community as it is led by the Spirit?** This is the type of question missional congregations must continually wrestle with as they engage the community and world.

TRINITARIAN MODEL

I hope it is evident that becoming a missional church does not mean forgoing a solid theological base. Congregations can be missional by living out a Trinitarian pattern. Congregations can make space for post–civil rights generations in the same way that God made spaces for individuals to play important roles in Israel's history and the lineage of Jesus. Congregations can collaborate with the post–civil rights generations in rethinking the structure or make-up of the believing community. Jesus collaborated with those outside of the power structures of the religious institution so that they would be visible. Congregations can develop a more holistic understanding of the Spirit that empowers individuals to communicate and act differently.

Becoming a missional church does not require throwing out the baby with the bath water. The same Trinitarian pattern that made the African American church vital during the Civil Rights era is still needed today. What has changed is the way in which the Trinitarian pattern is articulated and lived out in the congregation. Congregations that can maintain a solid theological grounding while rethinking the way the gospel is embodied will be vital. Congregations that believe embodying the gospel differently alters the heart of the gospel will continue to struggle. Missional congregations are committed to the gospel and to helping connect others to the gospel. Missional congregations are willing to rethink the way they make space for others, collaborate on the embodiment of the gospel, and seek a holistic understanding of the Spirit. Living this Trinitarian pattern requires rethinking certain practices of evangelism as I have discussed them in this chapter. These practices will be the topic of the next chapter.

REVISITING THE QUESTIONS

1. How can African American congregations make space so that the voices of all generations can be heard? What needs to change regarding leadership? (page 47)

2. Is your congregation willing to create a space for those who are truly seeking a relationship with God? Do you put God in a box? (page 51)

3. Why would I attend or become a part of a community where I am not valued? Name some things that make you feel appreciated! (page 59)

4. How can you invite individuals to be a part of your community if you cannot communicate with them? Do you understand hip hop, texting, and other forms of communication? Listen to some clean versions of Mos Def, and have youth share texting shorthand with you. (page 62)

5. How would your congregation be different if it acted boldly to construct community as it is led by the Spirit? Are you willing to be led by the Spirit? (page 64)

ACTIVITIES

1. Read Acts 2:1-13—Think about the verse (6) that focuses on hearing in one's own language.

2. Think of concrete ways the church can communicate with new generations in their language while maintaining the integrity of the gospel.

CHAPTER 4
NEW WINE

All right, stop what you are doing
'Cause I am about to ruin . . .[1]

Most African Americans above thirty remember the hit single "The Humpty Dance" by Digital Underground. The refrain to "stop what you are doing 'cause I am about to ruin" what we are used to is one that most of us recognize immediately. This refrain also speaks to African American congregations seeking to become missional. In this chapter, I argue it is time to "stop what you are doing, 'cause I am about to ruin" what we have come to accept in practicing evangelism. It is time to rethink how we engage in witnessing, hospitality, connectivity, and discipleship. While the practices themselves are essential, the way we do the practices needs to change. The Humpty Dance looked silly, but it got everyone out on the dance floor and moving. It is time congregations get everyone active and moving toward becoming missional.

IMPACT

Too many congregations are invisible or just blend into the landscape. People walk, drive, and jog by the church building, but do not see it as a place where things are happening.

Congregations have to produce new grapes or ideas that will help individuals to know there is life in the building. Staying inside of the building and thinking people have X-ray vision like Superman is not an option. This means people have to get outside of the building to make an impact on the community.

When reading Matthew, Mark, or Luke, it does not take long to figure out that Jesus is constantly going out from the temple to make some sort of impact on the community. Mark 1:29-34 tells how, after Jesus leaves the synagogue, he goes to the house of Simon and Andrew and heals Simon's mother-in-law. As you keep reading it tells about the people bringing the sick to Jesus to be healed. All of this happens outside of the synagogue. Jesus makes an impact on the community by going out and being in the community.

There are several African American congregations who are probably saying, "We go out and do things in the community!" Please do not stop these activities! The question is, **"How consistent is your witness in the community?"** Do you do activities once a year when you invite the same few neighbors to vacation Bible school? Do you make a flyer and shove it in mailboxes for the annual revival? Is your witness to the community consistent or intermittent?

Jesus' witness to the community was consistent. Jesus did not stay in the synagogue for 364 days and once a year check off his list "went outside into the community today." It is not possible to impact the community if it is not a consistent witness. Think about it from the perspective of those in the neighborhood. For 364 days the church shows no interest in their spiritual, social, or physical well-being and then it expects folk to show up because they left a flyer in the box. Would you?

African American congregations have to rethink how they are going to impact the community. This is especially true for those in the post-civil rights generations. What difference is your congregation's witnessing making in the community? The reason those in the Civil Rights and Black Consciousness generations flocked to African American congregations is they believed a difference was being made in the community (see chapter 2). The reason Jesus attracted so many individuals when he went out from the synagogue was folk believed a difference was going to be made in their lives.

One way to describe the difference being made by the earlier African American generations and Jesus is the ability to connect the spiritual, social, and physical well-being into a common vision. In chapter 2 I discussed how the Civil Rights and Black Consciousness generations developed a concrete vision of a society where blacks and whites were perceived as equals. African American congregations did all they could to support this vision. These congregations connected this vision to Jesus' ideal of the kingdom of God, where lives are not only altered in the future, but people start living differently in the present.

To reach the post–civil rights generations, congregations have to start re-imagining what it means to develop a vision that makes the ideal of the kingdom of God concrete. This is what happened in the New Testament as the gospel message got reinterpreted by Peter to Cornelius and eventually by Paul to the Gentiles. No longer was the gospel contained in one region, but like Jesus, Peter and Paul carried the gospel out to those who needed to hear it. Not only did they carry the gospel out, they helped people to see the big picture. For example, Cornelius understood inclusion in a new way after Peter, who was Jewish, entered into his house (Jews did not enter the houses of Gentiles). Finally, the encounters with others by Peter and Paul did not leave them the same. Peter rethought the meaning of holiness based upon his encounter with Cornelius.

We can rethink witnessing by taking the gospel out to the people, helping individuals to see the big picture, and developing an understanding that the encounter will not leave us the same. This is what Jesus did in proclaiming the kingdom of God. The idea of the kingdom of God was not something limited to the synagogue; it was for everyone. Because it was not limited to the synagogue, it was bigger than the synagogue. It was about the transformation of society. Even Jesus at times got reminded of how radical the idea of the kingdom was for society (as with Syrophoenician woman, Mark 7:26-30).

African American congregations have to develop a new mindset about witnessing that moves beyond an internal focus. The church is God's vessel for impacting society, but the church is not an end in itself. The goal is not to create members who get enamored with a building. **Are you enamored with your building?** The goal is to develop disciples seeking to go out and embody God's word. This means changing the way we witness to the post–civil rights generations. Congregations cannot think, "We have built it, they will come." The new mindset has to be "We must go out and find them."

Witnessing in this way can take many forms, but essential to all of these forms is authenticity. Simply trying to get people in the door to increase numbers is not valid. We should be witnessing to the power of the gospel to do something new in a person's life. It is not about getting new members and resources for the church; it is about pointing people to the good news of the gospel. The good news of the gospel is to be shared in word and deed.

What we are sharing with others is not our dream, but God's vision for society. Many in the post–civil rights generations are looking for a way to connect to something bigger than themselves. A quick listen to "New Day" by the hip hop violin duo Nuttin but Stringz is but one example of the post–civil rights generations putting in their own words this "something bigger." Sharing with this generation that God's vision is larger than any one church is a different way of witnessing for most congregations. The point is not to downplay the church, but to help individuals truly understand the role of the church in society. This is one of the reasons Jesus was so successful: it was never about Jesus' individual ministry. It was always about God's vision for society.

Finally, witnessing requires listening to those in the community. It is a collaborative effort that transforms all involved. The church should not dictate what the encounter with those in the post–civil rights generations will look like. Those in the post–civil rights generations have a voice if congregations are willing to listen. A part of witnessing is allowing outside voices to change our understanding of the gospel. Think about it. If you wanted information on what movies people under thirty are watching, it would make no sense to ask people over forty; rather, it would make sense to ask those under thirty what they are watching. Giving voice to those you are seeking means being prepared for some answers you may not want to hear.

Missional congregations get outside of their building and witness through word and deeds. This may take the form of taking care of the community by cleaning it up weekly or sponsoring conversations on hot topics at a local establishment. It is more than just doing specific acts, it is helping those in the post–civil rights generations understand how the words and deeds point to God's vision for the world. For example, a weekly clean-up of the community is grounded in God's vision of stewardship, which is a grander vision than any one congregation can claim. Most importantly, witnessing to the post–civil rights generations recognizes that they have ideas that are important to hear. Someone may already have started a community recycling program, so instead of ignoring what is happening the church works with the current program, always remembering the big picture of stewardship.

Missional congregations are intentional about how they impact the community. They understand it has to be an on-going witness and not a one-time event. The goal is to be the church in a different way that is not focused on putting warm bodies in seats. The goal is to embody something different that is visible to those outside of the congregation.

INVITATION

Inviting people to participate in God's work is just as important as impacting the community through witnessing. The truth is the witnessing itself should be a form of invitation. People want to get involved because they perceive an openness by those witnessing to them. When Jesus healed someone the person often immediately followed Jesus (for instance Matthew 20:29-34). Jesus' witness was an invitation to be a part of something new.

One of the strengths of the Civil Rights and Black Consciousness generations is they were inviting individuals to become a part of something new. The focus was not on building up a particular congregation, it was on transforming society. The invitation was not restricted. All were welcome to participate in moving toward something new. African American congregations have to rethink the practice of invitation from the perspective of the on-going work of transformation, never forgetting this is done under the guidance of the Holy Spirit.

In Matthew 4:18-22, when Jesus calls Peter and Andrew it is not to build up his particular synagogue. Jesus calls them so that they can invite others to become a part of something new. The two disciples are called to embody a new understanding of the kingdom of God that is inclusive of all individuals. The invitation is communicated in such a way that it makes sense, but it is also big enough to require leaving their profession and following after Jesus. It is an invitation to a new way of life.

Take note that Jesus' invitations are never coercive. Jesus does not beat people up or demean them to get them to follow. Jesus will describe the costs for following. For example, Jesus tells the rich young man (Matthew 19:21) to sell all his possessions, give the money to the poor, and then to come follow. Jesus describes the costs for being a follower, but never coerces the young man to follow. We have to be careful when inviting not to be coercive or judgmental. We are the extenders of the invitation and not the determiners of the outcome of the invitation. **Are there ways you can invite others without making them feel uncomfortable?**

African American congregations seeking to rethink the way they invite the post–civil rights generations to participate in God's work have to re-interpret their understanding of hospitality. Beyond separating the invitation from the response to the invitation, these congregations will need to do the following.

First, invite in language that those being invited can understand. Be patient! It may take repeated invitations before an invitation is accepted, so having the patience to keep inviting is important. Not only is patience important, but creating a space for those being invited is essential. This is a sign of true hospitality.

The story of Pentecost is memorable for many reasons. One of the things that happened at Pentecost is individuals were able to hear what was said in their own language. There was no need for a translator because they were hearing the message in their own language. When we think of the best practices of missionaries taking the gospel to other places, those who are able to communicate in the indigenous language often receive a better hearing. This should not be a surprise since we all think and process within a particular cultural context.

Communicating with and inviting those in the post–civil rights generations needs to be in language familiar to them. This is a form of hospitality. The responsibility is on those embodying the gospel and doing the inviting to have an understanding of the appropriate language for that context. Putting the responsibility on the other person is an easy move to make and one that we all do. It sounds like this: "The reason the post–civil rights generations are not in church is because they have no spirituality." It is always about the other person and never our own reluctance to be hospitable.

Taking the time to learn the language or languages of those in the post–civil rights generations will be challenging and frustrating at times. If we are serious, however, about seeking their presence in the church, then we must learn their language. This does not mean not keeping it real and trying to be something one is not. It means having a fluency in the culture in which the post–civil rights generations live and operate. Hospitality is about making the outsider comfortable and welcome. This requires knowing something about their culture and not assuming they are just like you.

Hospitality means developing an understanding of how to invite and having the patience to stick with it. Most of us are familiar with the game Monopoly. What many of us do not know is that when Charles Darrow first pitched the game to Parker Brothers it was turned down. Darrow did not give up, and Monopoly is one of the top-selling board games of all times. Patience! Congregations often try something one time and, if it does not go well, they give up. For example, a congregation sponsors a back-to-school bash and very few people show up. Some in the congregation are ready to kill the idea because it did not produce the desired results.

This is understandable, but patience is a part of hospitality. Continuing to extend an invitation to the outsider is critical. Jesus is asked (Matthew 18:21-22), "How many times should you forgive?" Jesus' response is, "Not seven times, but seventy-seven!" I am adapting Jesus' response to say, "Invite seventy-seven times!" **Where are some of the places you can be more patient in extending an invitation to outsiders?** A part of what it means to be the church is grounded in inviting outsiders to experience something new. Congregations cannot become impatient when they are not getting the desired results.

Hospitality requires not strictly focusing on results and remembering it may take a while for those invited to believe it's sincere. This is especially true for congregations who have not been inviting outsiders to come. Think about it! If a golf club in town that previously excluded women members all of a sudden started inviting women to join, how would they respond? Many of the women would be hesitant and wonder what had changed. It might take multiple invitations and seeing the golf club embody a new attitude toward women before individuals took them seriously. Congregations seeking those in the post–civil rights generations have to extend multiple invitations and embody a new attitude to be taken seriously.

Finally, hospitality means creating a space in the congregation for those coming in to feel comfortable. In chapter 3 I discussed the importance of space for the post–civil rights generations. This is an extension of that conversation. Hospitality requires making space for those you are inviting. This is especially true in worship. When individuals come and visit a church we tend to think about hospitality as the way they are greeted and how friendly the congregation is. Certainly this is a part of hospitality, but only a part.

The worship experience itself reflects how open the congregation is to outsiders. Many readers will have two immediate responses to altering worship. First, "Why should we alter worship when no one from that generation is coming?" Second, "Our worship reflects who we are as a congregation!" Let me begin with the latter claim. It is important for the worship experience to be authentic or it will have little meaning. Worship can be authentic, however, and still be different than it is currently.

For example, involving different worship participants and reading different Bible translations are two simple steps. Making sure there is not a lot of dead space in the worship experience is important. This means thinking about how you transition from one part of the worship experience to another part and not having people just sitting. More radical changes include thinking about the style of music and offering a broader repertoire. Think through the components of the worship experience and how to help those from a post–civil rights generation make sense of what is happening.

Altering worship is a challenge, but hospitality requires making the outsider feel welcome. Think about it! The reason many of you are at your current congregation is you feel comfortable in worship. The worship experience spoke to you in a meaningful manner. **How do you make sure those in the post–civil rights generations have this same experience?** This is not putting down tradition. It is thinking about how certain traditions speak to the current context.

In fact, contrary to belief, many in the post–civil rights generations are not anti-tradition. They are constantly borrowing from older generations in music, styles, and other areas of life and putting their own spin on things. For example, someone like Usher borrows from James Brown and emulates his moves. Congregations should work collaboratively with those in the post–civil rights generations on interpreting traditions and not perceive those in the post generations as oppositional.

The other issue is, "Why should we alter worship when no one is coming?" No one may be coming because you have not altered worship. Congregations, like restaurants, develop reputations that can stick with them. When you go to a restaurant and receive bad service you often tell others and do not return. The hospitality is not up to par. Congregations not willing to think differently about worship develop a reputation of not being hospitable toward certain individuals.

It becomes a self-fulfilling prophecy that no one is coming and the congregation is caught in a vicious circle. The reputation of the congregation precedes it. Individuals avoid the congregation because of the reputation. The congregation sees no need to change because no one from the post–civil rights generations is coming. Breaking this circle requires changing the public perception of the congregation, which means rethinking hospitality.

There is a difference in saying we will do it and doing it. If one's favorite sports team was in last place the previous year, but announces it is going to win the championship the next year, it does not make them champions. Simply stating they are going to win the championship is not going to be convincing. When they go out and sign new players who are talented and change their overall philosophy, it is more convincing. When they actually win games, it is even more convincing. Congregations have to do more than talk about changing. They have to make changes that let outsiders know something new is happening.

Hospitality is a critical component of invitation. Hospitality includes the language in which we communicate, being patient when we do not see immediate results, and making space for those we are inviting. Although we talked about witnessing as a separate practice, the truth is witnessing and hospitality work hand in hand. The way we witness is a part of how we extend hospitality. Those in the post–civil rights generations develop a perception about a congregation based upon the way individuals witness to them. Hospitality has to be a part of witnessing.

IGNITE

Missional congregations connect people with God.[2] They ignite a flame in people that propels them to seek a deeper understanding of and relationship with God. The goal of developing this relationship is discipleship. A disciple is a true follower of Jesus. Peter and Andrew accepted the invitation to go with Jesus and then spent the next three years learning what it meant to be a follower of Jesus. Most congregations believe they exist to make followers of Jesus, but often operate differently in practice. The focus is on membership and not discipleship.

Traditionally, a person visits a congregation and eventually becomes a member of that faith community. Some congregations have classes for new members and the expectation is once the person becomes a member they will be active in the congregation. The focus is on membership. Most churches respond to the question, "How large is your congregation?" by naming the "members" on the church roll. For example, a congregation will say we have 150 on the church roll, but usually 70 in worship. The measuring stick is the number on the roll, even though only about 50 percent actually are in worship during the week.

Why is church membership so important? Does membership have its privileges? The old American Express ad told us that membership has its privileges. The implication is that becoming a member means you get something others are not getting. In congregations we often operate with this same mentality. Because I am a member of "Evergreen Community Church" I have a guaranteed spot in heaven. Some of us equate church membership with eternal life. One is challenged to find a place in the Bible where church membership is equated with eternal life. Certainly there is a connection to being a follower of Jesus and this is best achieved in community. There is a difference between the way we think about membership and being in community together.

On a practical level some feel that one of the privileges of membership is it gives them the right to make decisions that benefit them. Congregations develop policies that benefit certain members in the congregation: for example, a burial policy that guarantees certain families get plots for free because they were founding members of the congregation. I am not putting down founding members of a congregation. I am suggesting the focus on membership detracts from creating followers of Jesus because it pushes a congregation to be self-absorbed.

One of the things Jesus constantly fought against was this idea of privilege. Scripture often depicts the Pharisees and scribes as thinking they were special because of their role in the temple and religious community. They were this special club of members. In John 8:31-47, Jesus debates some in the Jewish hierarchy about the meaning of discipleship. In verse 33 those Jesus is debating respond that they are descendants of Abraham, trying to make a special claim against Jesus. Jesus turns this statement against them by explaining what it really means to be a descendant of Abraham. Jesus implies that all are children of Abraham or connected to Abraham. Membership does not have its privileges in the kingdom of God.

For congregations seeking those in the post–civil rights generations this means developing a new mindset. The focus should not be on membership, but on connecting people to Christ. What binds the community together is not a sense of privilege, but a rootedness in Jesus. The measuring stick becomes the ability of the faith community to connect people to Jesus so that their lives can be transformed. Moreover, the faith community must learn to walk with people as their lives are being transformed by the Holy Spirit. The focus is on vitality. **Does your congregation focus on membership or vitality?** Let me be clear that vitality is not oppositional to growth. In reality, vital congregations are often growing.

There is a difference between focusing on membership and vitality. The goal is not simply to make one a member of a congregation. The goal keeps the big picture in mind of connecting people to God by walking with them as they become followers of Jesus. The congregation is a means to the end of making people followers of Christ. The congregation, however, is not the end itself, which often happens when the focus is on membership.

The reason this is important for those in the post–civil rights generations is that our culture thinks in terms of connectivity. We are connected through Facebook, Youtube, and all kinds of wireless devices. It is through these connections that many people form community. A missional congregation that focuses on connectivity is interested in the way individuals become followers of Jesus. A person who is committed to coming to worship, attends a faith development opportunity, and embodies the gospel outside the doors of the church is not looked down upon just because she or he is not a member.

Missional congregations seek to ignite a flame in people to develop a deeper relationship with Jesus. They are interested in touching and changing lives. The goal is for the congregation to become a community where all generations can be connected to God and one another. Rethinking igniting lives from the perspective of connectivity means congregations can participate in God's work of transformation without worrying about one's membership status. A missional congregation is bound by rootedness in Jesus and not other ancillary connections.

NEW WINE

New wine represents the new mindset that is needed to re-think evangelistic practices. Missional congregations must impact the community through intentional witnessing. Missional congregations must invite others to participate by extending hospitality. Missional congregations must ignite a flame in individuals to become connected to God. Many of you are saying these ideas do not represent a new mindset; they are all biblically based. Those making this claim are right!

All of the practices discussed in this chapter are things Jesus did and taught others to do. In fact, these practices were in the fabric of many African American congregations for years. The challenge is reinterpreting these ideas for the post–civil rights generations who have a different cultural context from those in the Civil Rights and Black Consciousness generations. The work of reinterpreting requires a new mindset that can look at the biblical text and the cultural context in fresh ways. This is why collaborating with those in the post–civil rights generations is so important. They bring a fresh set of eyes!

Missional congregations are willing to try and do different things like collaborating with those they are trying to reach. One thing is certain. Nothing is going to change if the congregation is not willing to be transformed by the Holy Spirit. **Is your congregation willing to be transformed by the Holy Spirit?** This means praying to God for guidance. I did not talk about prayer in each section of this chapter, but prayer should ground everything a congregation is doing. A congregation cannot impact, invite, or ignite if it is not praying on how to do so.

Too often congregations proceed with plans before praying about the direction they are going. This gets to the heart of this chapter and the point of developing a new mindset. The church is God's instrument for reaching others. When the church forgets its role then the focus shifts to bringing people to a building. If your congregation did not have a building, then could you still impact the community, invite through hospitality, and ignite others to connect to God? I hope the answer is yes! If it is no or we do not know, then it is certainly time for a new mindset.

REVISITING THE QUESTIONS

1. How consistent is your witness in the community? Are you a drive-in-for-Sunday-service-and-Bible-study congregation? (page 68)

2. Are you enamored with your building? Does the physical building represent what it means to be a church for your congregation? (page 70)

3. Are there ways you can invite others without making them feel uncomfortable? What kinds of invitations are welcoming to you? (page 73)

4. Where are some of the places you can be more patient in extending an invitation to outsiders? (page 75)

5. How do you make sure those in the post-civil rights generations have this same experience? What would happen if the worship service looked different? (page 77)

6. Why is church membership so important? Does membership have its privileges? (page 79)

7. Does your congregation focus on membership or vitality? What do you perceive to be the difference between these two ideas? (page 80)

8. Is your congregation willing to be transformed by the Holy Spirit? (page 82)

ACTIVITIES

1. Read Mark 1:29-34—Jesus leaves the "building" and goes out in the community.

2. Think of concrete things you can do monthly outside of the building in the community.

CHAPTER 5
A BETTER WINESKIN

I wanna go where the mountains are
high enough to echo my song . . .
I wanna go where the stars shine
bright enough to show me the way[1]

One of the questions frequently asked is, "How do we do it?" How do we get there? Like in the lyrics above by India Arie, we know where we want to go. The problem is getting to that place. Many of us use a map when we are not certain where we are headed. No one map can capture every possibility for traveling to a destination. The truth is, no one map will work for every congregation. Congregations seeking a one-map-fits-all solution are in trouble! If my goal is to drive to Kansas City, then the map only helps me if I know where I am starting because that will determine the direction I am driving. It makes a difference whether one begins in California or New York.

Once we know the starting point, we can pick the route we want to travel to our destination. This chapter is a missional map. It is not the only way to get to the destination, but it is a way. This chapter pulls together the theological insights and evangelistic practices covered previously to help congregations develop a better wineskin that engages the cultural shift. This chapter will help congregations toward their destination, but it is only a map and not a step by step solution.

GETTING STARTED

Pastor Sharp kept clicking the pen on and off nervously. On and off! On and off! They were having a church meeting in a few minutes to discuss their future. Renewal Community Church used to be vibrant and well known throughout the city. But the neighborhood changed. The people were older and tired. They did see a few young people, but not many. Each year there were fewer and fewer people in worship. Everyone kept waiting for God to wave a magic wand and return them back to glory. As each year went by the congregation kept dwindling and no rabbit was ever pulled out of a hat. Pastor Sharp just kept working that pen. On and off! On and off!

Do you recognize this congregation? It was strong and vibrant forty or fifty years ago, but is now struggling to maintain itself. Unfortunately too many congregations resemble this picture when they look in the mirror. Too many of these congregations are waiting for God to wave a magic wand and to return them to their glory days. Fortunately (or some may believe unfortunately) that is not the way God works, so we have to participate with God (follow God's lead) in moving toward a new future that embraces kingdom living. There are many ways to move forward, so let's return to the story and find out what Renewal Community Church plans to do.

Pastor Sharp was still clicking the pen on and off when the meeting started. Pastor Sharp exclaimed, "We have been going around and around the past few years about what we need to do. And we all know we need to do something! Well it is time we stop talking and actually do something! I have gone to several workshops this year with many of you, and the one thing that seems clear is we must begin to pray!" Sister Johnson interrupted, "Pastor, we pray every day. That does not sound like any sort of plan to me." Pastor Sharp replied, "We do pray every day, but we are going to be more intentional in the way we pray for the next few weeks."

Congregations seeking to change need to be intentional about how they pray. A group of dedicated people from the congregation should begin to pray for direction from God.[2] All congregations should want to grow and be vibrant. Too often congregations try to do this by human effort. Congregations try program after program to turn their church around and cannot figure out why it is not working. These congregations forgot to be intentional about prayer and communicating with the one person who can transform their future—God. God does this not by any hocus pocus, but by working through us.

Martha Grace Reese quotes from a pastor in her book about the impact of prayer on the church. The pastor says:

> Prayer is a HUGE thing here. We have a prayer action team that's a group committed to fasting and praying. They undergird every thing we do. You almost can't talk about it as a separate thing because the prayer is right there all the time. It has changed everything. Prayer makes openings, and we see possibilities and shifts and openings happening all the time. Now that I think about it, we really assume the Spirit's going to be leading.[3]

Congregations seeking transformation have to "assume the Spirit is going to be leading." As the pastor explains, "It changes everything." By *everything* this pastor meant that the congregation started to embody something new that was contagious inside and out.

How many of our congregations exude a positive, contagious spirit inside and out? If we are honest in the way we pray, then it means we are opening ourselves up for God to take us in God's direction, which may be a new direction for us. It may not seem like much is being accomplished immediately, but a visible transformation will occur in the life of the church through prayer. Our foreparents would gather whenever they could for prayer because they knew God could change their circumstances. We have to be just as intentional as our foreparents and pray without ceasing for direction from God.

Let me be clear that God's communication will not come to just one person, but will manifest itself corporately. Certainly one person may have a vision from God of how the congregation should move forward, but God will also help others to catch glimpses of the vision. This discernment process is important because God is calling not just one or two people forward from the congregation, but the entire body. The body as a whole has to take ownership of God's plan for moving forward.

HAVING FAITH

Renewal Community Church had been in prayer for six weeks and something was starting to happen. More and more people were talking about changing the structure of leadership and worship. Pastor Sharp was cautiously excited. Renewal had been down this path before and the wheels started coming off. Trying to keep the wheels on this time was going to take more prayer and a real willingness to start moving in a different direction.

The biggest battle was going to be over worship. The worship expe-rience had not drastically changed in forty years at Renewal. Some of the mature members disagreed and pointed out the new songs the church sang off of the radio. This was not new, though, because the church always sang the latest hits off of the radio. The truth is, a visi-tor to the church in 1968 would have a hard time seeing how the serv-ice was different today.

We are all afraid of change! The truth is we all like stability in our lives. There is something comforting about being able to count on certain things like our faith. When people suggest things need to change it feels like a personal attack on us and God. **Does the word *change* scare you? Do you feel personally attacked when others suggest you need to change?**

Congregations have to change and be agents of change, because God is always doing a new thing. The culture is always changing, and this means the church has to examine how it is communicat-ing with those in the culture. This does not mean the church suc-cumbs to the culture or is no longer set apart from the culture, but it does mean the church is aware of the cultural shifts. For exam-ple, the Civil Rights and Black Consciousness generations are aware that the post–civil rights generations think about and often live out their faith differently. Simply ignoring this fact or hoping that the post–civil rights generations will become the mirror image of their generations is not a good solution.

What is it that really has to change? How much change is enough? These are the questions many congregations are asking. Do we have to change the leadership structure of the church? Do we have to change our attitudes? If we add a youth choir, "Is that enough change?" If we add a contemporary worship, "Is that enough change?" All of these are things that may or may not change. One thing that has to change is being discussed by Pastor Sharp with a few members at Renewal.

Pastor Sharp was cornered by a couple of the good saints. They were questioning, more like interrogating, the pastor about "things in the air." One saint exclaimed, "Pastor, is it true that you are getting ready to make some major changes?" Before the pastor could respond, the other saint chimed in, "You are not getting ready to mess with worship, are you?" Both saints added, almost in unison, "The last pastor who tried that did not last too long." Before the saints could get another word in, Pastor Sharp said while squirming out of the corner, "I hope you both will read Luke 17:5-6."

I hope you will read Luke 17:5-6. Why would Pastor Sharp reference this particular text? Pastor Sharp recognizes that conversations like the one above are grounded in fear of change and not living out our faith. Faith is one of those words we often talk about but never apply to our own situations. If you ask a seasoned Christian what faith is, the quick response is, "The substance of things hoped for, the evidence of things not seen" (Hebrews 11:1). Individuals in congregations know the rote answer, but what is the evidence of living out this answer?

In Luke 17:5-6, Jesus suggests that if you have just a little bit of faith (faith of a mustard seed), then mountains can be moved. A part of disliking change is the discomfort of not knowing what to expect. However, a big part of disliking change is the risk involved. When we have done something the same way for a long time, it requires a big risk and energy to do something differently. Taking a risk requires faith. Jesus admonishes us, "It requires the faith of a mustard seed." We cannot know with certainty the outcome when we are risking (stepping out on faith), but we do know the mountains will **not** move if we **do not** move out of our comfort zone.

Congregations seeking to be missional have to be willing to step out on faith. Change is never easy, but not changing probably means moving toward non-existence. **Can you think of a time when you stepped out on faith? What helped you to make such a courageous decision?** Congregations willing to step out on faith find that God's safety net is huge. Even when we feel like we are falling, God's net is there to catch us.

Let me be clear that stepping out on faith does not mean God's plan for our congregation is the same as our plan for the congregation. It may be that the role our congregation plays is giving our resources to another church that can more effectively do ministry in the community. This seems harsh and is what we fear most, but the goal is not the survival of our congregation. The goal is doing our part for the kingdom, which means being selfless and not selfish. Congregations that are selfish continue to be only inward focused and have lost sight of their calling from God.

MAKING SPACE: PREPARING A PLACE AT THE TABLE

Pastor Sharp was pleasantly surprised by how well things were progressing at Renewal. The congregation was continuing to be prayerful and a consensus was forming about stepping out on faith. Pastor Sharp knew the congregation was not out of the woods yet. In fact, some of the mature saints from the Civil Rights and Black Consciousness generations wanted to meet. Pastor Sharp was sure it was because of a proposal to be prepared for new guests. Pastor Sharp picked up a pen from his desk and headed to the meeting—clicking the pen on and off, on and off.

Before Pastor Sharp could settle in a seat, one of the saints asked, "Is it true you are up to something related to our mission statement?" Pastor Sharp paused a minute, then replied, "If by up to something you mean printing the statement in the bulletin and posting it in a prominent place, then yes! Our mission is to 'Impact the community with the love of God, Invite people to Christ, and Ignite disciples with the transforming power of the Spirit.' I want us to be intentional in living out our mission."

Living out the mission of the congregation is essential. Most congregations have a mission statement that encourages them to be outward focused while not ignoring the inward work of developing disciples. The challenge is actually embodying the mission statement. For example, Renewal's mission statement is outward focused because it begins with impacting the community, but it is also inward focused because it seeks to ignite disciples. The congregation is intentional in maintaining a healthy balance between those outside the walls and those needing to grow on the journey. Most congregations tend to focus on the inward work and are not outward focused. They ignore or downplay the part about impacting the community. This translates into an attitude of protectionism. Individuals feel like they have ownership over the church and what the church does.

If we take the mission of the church seriously, then that should shift how we think about newcomers. As we live out the mission, it helps us to prepare a space for others to enter into the life of the congregation. Congregations should always be seeking to be in relationship with new people and the gifts those individuals bring to the life of the community. Imagine a dinner party with people sitting and eating, but a few of the seats are empty. When those individuals finally arrive and take their seats they see everything is already set for them. They can come eat and become a part of the conversation without worrying about finding utensils, a plate, or a glass. Congregations seeking to be missional are called to set a place at the table for those who will be coming to join them. They should not have the dishes hidden in a cabinet where they are the only ones with a key!

We have to be intentional about preparing a space for those who will be coming to join us. We have to change our attitude from one of protectionism to welcoming the gifts others bring. **How is your congregation setting a place at the table for others to come join you?** This is an important question for your congregation to struggle with as it moves toward becoming missional.

ENGAGING THE COMMUNITY

It was noisy, extremely noisy! But Pastor Sharp was excited. Renewal was hosting a "Getting to know our neighbors" block party. What made this day even more perfect was that many of the mature saints had brought the idea forward. A few had said, "We tried that before and it did not work." But even before the pastor could speak, others chimed in and reminded those with doubts that this was a new day for the congregation. The turnout was not massive, but it was still impressive. The joy on the faces of the young and old laughing, playing, and having a good time together was priceless.

One of the toughest challenges for all congregations is figuring out how to reach out. If the congregation has been inward focused, then it is likely that reaching out will not be natural. Congregations in this boat have to be intentional about letting the community know they exist, they care, and that they seek to be in relationship. This is not a "one event and done" effort.

Many congregations do a version of the block party that Renewal is doing to reconnect with the community, and when the folk do not show up on Sunday, they say, "See, I told you!"

We have to remember that the people in the neighborhood, young and old, are just like that person who, at one point, was in relationship with us but drifted away. When they come back seeking relationship again the tendency is to be cautious because we remember the previous experience. For congregations to think one event will change everything that has come before is shortsighted. It will be an on-going process that involves give and take. Those who are not currently a part of the congregation have no guarantee that the church will not just disappear again. It is important not to think one and done. The reality is the congregation is going to have a lot of work in front of it. Pastor Sharp describes some of this work in a conversation after the block party.

"WE TOLD YOU SO, PASTOR! Only two people showed up on Sunday and they were not in the post–civil rights generations. We spent all that money and have nothing to show for it." Pastor Sharp was prepared for the criticism. Pastor Sharp responded, "Let's not jump to conclusions. Remember this is the first time in years Renewal has connected with many in the post–civil rights generations. It is going to take time and a lot of relationship-building. We already have the next event planned, thanks to some good conversation and an invitation between some of you and one of the community representatives." The saint who had chastised the pastor asked, "What is it and will it cost more money?" Pastor Sharp responded, "It is an old skool and nu skool dialogue, and the costs are minimal."

Impacting the community takes time. Being an invitational congregation seeking to impact the community is essential. Letting those in the community and especially those in the post–civil rights generations know that the congregation is willing to make space for them is a big step. It also is a very tough step. Opening up the channels of communication and keeping a dialogue going with those who are open in the community is necessary.

Becoming a missional congregation means being intentional about creating these types of dialogues. It is about bridging the gap between the generations so they can really hear each other and not talk around or over each other. Each side makes assumptions about the other side that may or may not be true. It is only when a real dialogue begins that some of the barriers can start coming down. Let's look in on the third *old skool* and *nu skool* dialogue at Renewal.

A young woman who lived in the neighborhood and one of the seasoned saints of the church were up front sharing an idea with the others. The young woman said, "We want to start an old skool and nu skool study group. The younger folk would be responsible for presenting the old skool portion and the more seasoned people would present the nu skool part." The seasoned saint chimed in, "For the first one we thought it would be fun to have the post–civil rights generations read Marvin Gaye lyrics and the Civil Rights and Black Consciousness generations read Lauryn Hill lyrics." What do you all think?"

What do you think? How is your congregation intentional about bridging the gap between the various generations? This is a bold step for Renewal, doing a study that moves many of them out of their comfort zone and is not centered on the Bible in the traditional manner. Think about it. By doing the study Renewal continues to be invitational and to make space for those in the post–civil rights and other generations. This will also impact the community, because as others hear of the openness of the congregation to engage in authentic dialogue it will pique their interest.

Consider Paul when he began his discourse about an unknown God as a way of bridging the gap between cultures. Certainly Paul was trying to persuade in his speech and he was not addressing a generational difference. What is similar is that Paul recognized his listeners would hear him differently if he showed some familiarity with their context. Bridging the gap between generations requires some recognition of their context. Being a missional congregation means building this bridge. Congregations that are able to do this with integrity will see a visible change inside the four walls and outside in the community.

KEEPING IT REAL

Pastor Sharp was astounded at the turnout. They had to move the study to the sanctuary because so many had come. The old skool and nu skool dialogue had gone well, so they decided to do a world religions conversation. Pastor Sharp knew this was going to be a touchy topic with the Renewal congregation, but it also offered them an opportunity for real honest dialogue. So many people have questions about the differences between religions, and taking those questions seriously was important.

As discussed in chapter 3, many post–civil rights individuals have a lot of questions about religion. They are not automatically just going to agree that Christianity is the one and only option. Being in conversation in an honest way with them is important for them to perceive the congregation in a different light. This does not mean denying or watering down one's beliefs, but it does mean engaging tough questions.

If the only way congregations can persuade individuals to begin a Christian journey is through fear or hammering them over the head, then the church will continue to struggle. Congregations are called to witness to God's providence, the presence of Jesus, and the working of the Holy Spirit. This does not require fear or hammering someone over the head. The truth is, many individuals in congregations have had and continue to have questions that they are afraid to voice. As Renewal is about to learn, keeping it real does not necessarily scare people away; it may draw them closer.

Pastor Sharp was preparing to start the world religion dialogue that focused on Islam this week when a seasoned saint asked to speak. Pastor Sharp was nervous because this saint was very critical of the dialogue and had let everyone know so in no uncertain terms. Pastor Sharp nodded and yielded the floor to the saint. The saint spoke, "I want to testify today. I have never told anyone this, but my uncle was active in the Nation of Islam when I was a teenager. He would take me to some of the rallies and I have to say they were exciting. I never heard Malcolm X in person, but the ones I did hear were convincing. I have always been ashamed of going to those meetings since becoming a Christian because I did not want anyone to know about my past, but these conversations have helped me to see things differently. I want to thank the pastor and the young folk for opening my eyes."

The stories that are in most congregations are varied and incredible. We often do not think about sharing our story until someone helps us see things in a different way. It is our stories that make us really human, and the sharing of the stories helps us keep it real. There is such a thing as too much sharing. Some things should not be shared in a large group. But some stories can be invitational and help further dialogue and help outsiders to feel like insiders.

The power of stories is they can be challenging and invitational at the same time. This is what makes the gospel so compelling. The gospel tells the story of God's relationship with humanity in a way that challenges us to live differently and invites us to share the majesty of God's grace with others. The gospel opens our eyes to a different way of existing in the world that we had not imagined previously. This requires keeping it real and not pretending like we have all the answers or have it all together.

When you are invested in something, nothing is worse than feeling attacked or like someone is diminishing its value. Keeping it real means a willingness to let others question what we believe in an authentic way without becoming defensive. There is a difference between seeking a deeper understanding and denigrating someone. Many times when people are exploring their faith it is because they are seeking a deeper understanding and it is not about denigrating others. Becoming a missional congregation means keeping it real and maintaining a willingness to engage tough issues and questions.

MAKING SPACE: OUTSIDERS BECOME INSIDERS

Pastor Sharp could hardly believe the difference at Renewal. The congregation had a new energy and vitality. The congregation was becoming missional. Pastor Sharp realized they still had some issues to deal with. They were getting ready to incorporate some new elements in worship and some of the seasoned saints would start complaining. Pastor Sharp realized it was time to move forward and not to give in to fear.

One of the most sacred cows is worship. Congregations will often agree to make some changes as long as worship stays the same. To really make space in the congregation for post–civil rights generations, the worship experience often needs to change. Allowing the voices of all generations to be heard in worship is important. The question is, **"What is it that someone takes away from your worship experience?"** Is it simply an emotional high and ten minutes later a person remember nothing from the encounter with the Holy?

All of us should experience God at a deeper level in worship, should learn something in worship, and should be challenged in worship. There is no one way to experience God, and a worship experience should provide space for a variety of ways to connect with God. For example, some people do it through music, others do it through silence, others do it through visual arts, and some need to be physically active. Depending on one's worship preference, having to experience other ways of engaging God can be annoying. We must remember that worship is for the whole community to experience God and not just us!

We should learn or take something away from worship. We should have a new insight into what it means to be in relationship with God and our neighbor after leaving worship. This insight is not incompatible with a high-spirited worship experience. This insight is critical for those in the post–civil rights generations who are wondering, "What difference does this worship experience make for my life?" If worship is not making a difference, then why should outsiders come be a part of it?

The typical answer is because people should be concerned about their salvation. Yes! Salvation is important, but depending on your circumstances that may not be where you enter the journey. Someone experiencing hell on earth will not think about damnation in the same manner as someone with a different reality. Both individuals need to be able to take something away from worship that is meaningful.

We should always be challenged in worship to be missional Christians. We should not come to worship and leave week after week never feeling challenged to live out God's word in new ways. Worship is not a social meeting! Worship should prepare us to go out and re-present Jesus to the world. This is what made worship during the Civil Rights and Black Consciousness generations so powerful. It is what African American congregations have to reclaim for the post–civil rights generations—the idea that worship prepares us to engage the world in a new way, a Christ way! What does this actually look like in worship? Let's listen in as a few saints at Renewal discuss some of the changes.

Pastor Sharp was sitting in the office with the door open and recognized the voices of a few members discussing some of the worship changes. The one saint was thrilled by some of the changes. She really liked the way the choir started singing "Amazing Grace" as a traditional hymn, then switched to singing it as a contemporary song, and ended with a young person rapping the words while the choir hummed in the background. She said, "I felt the Spirit moving during that song!"

The other saint was concerned about the pastor getting input from the congregation on the sermons. She was complaining that some of the folk giving input were not members! She was doubly concerned that the pastor was allowing feedback on the sermons on Facebook! She said, "Folk who don't even know the Bible commenting on what the pastor preached. I have never seen such a thing!" The first saint replied, "The young folk seem to pay more attention and are sharing what they learn with their friends."

Creating a worship experience that bridges the gap between generations takes a lot of work. It can be done with creativity and a lot of planning. At Renewal they did not stop singing hymns, but found a way to expand the way the hymns were communicated. The hope is to deepen the worship experience. The idea of allowing individuals to inform the sermon challenges people to start making connections between the culture and the Bible. Most importantly, the ability to respond to the sermon not only helps to make disciples but, depending on the medium of response, encourages sharing.

Becoming a missional congregation means making space in worship for all generations to feel comfortable and challenged to live out the gospel. **Does your worship experience create this type of space?** One way to find out is to talk with the various generations and to find out how they perceive worship. This may require inviting someone in to observe worship if a particular generation is missing, but the feedback will be invaluable. Collaborating with all generations to do something authentic that deepens worship, allows individuals to take something away, and challenges them to re-present the gospel has to be kept front and center.

MARKERS

When we are unsure of where we are traveling, it is common to look for markers along the way to make sure we are going in the right direction. There are some markers for a missional map also. First, the congregation understands the importance of and commits to undergirding the journey with prayer. If the congregation is not willing to commit to praying or does so in a lackluster manner, then the congregation is headed in the wrong direction.

Second, the congregation starts to exhibit a new energy. This means individuals in the congregation are buying into becoming missonal and are living it out visibly. I must caution that not everyone in the congregation is going to buy into becoming missional. There are some individuals who would rather die than be transformed. When a consensus forms it will transform the congregation in spite of those who do not want to move forward.

Third, the congregation will stop being so inward focused. A congregation that is seeking to be missional begins to engage the community and make space for them within the body. An inward-focused congregation tends to gather for worship and possibly Bible study, but has no interest in doing anything that does not maintain its survival. Becoming a missional congregation means not focusing on survival and focusing on thriving. A vital congregation is one that is truly the bread of life to the community because it is where people come to be fed.

Fourth, the congregation is willing to change. Becoming a missional congregation requires making some changes to reach out to the post–civil rights generations. Congregations that are willing to be transformed by the Holy Spirit are on their way to becoming missional. Congregations unwilling to do anything different, who want everything to stay the same, are headed in the wrong direction. The objective is not to force change, but it is to be transformed in such a way that individuals can truly see it is a work of God.

One last caution! Anyone who has travelled with children knows their favorite saying, "Are we there yet?" The journey to becoming a missional congregation by connecting with the post–civil rights generations will make some people anxious and they will begin to ask, "Are we there yet?" Of course the appropriate response is, "No, not yet!" The journey will seem long, but like all journeys, just when you think you will never make it, you see a sign that says, "Destination ahead." Do not give up!

REVISITING THE QUESTIONS

1. Does the word *change* scare you? Do you feel personally attacked when others suggest you need to change? (page 89)

2. Can you think of a time when you stepped out on faith? What helped you to make such a courageous decision? (page 91)

3. How is your congregation setting a place at the table for others to come join you? What are you doing to make outsiders feel at home? (page 93)

4. What is it that someone takes away from your worship experience? What difference does worship make in one's life three days down the road? (page 99)

5. Does your worship experience create a welcoming space? What needs to change so that the post–civil rights generations feel comfortable in worship? (page 101)

ACTIVITIES

1. Read Hebrews 11:1-2—Think about whether we really believe that those things not seen can happen.

2. Make a list of things that will require a leap of faith for the congregation to move forward. Start praying for God's discernment about this list.

CONCLUSION

Obstacles are inefficient, follow your intuition, free your inner soul and break away from tradition.[1]

Some of you will recognize the lyrics above from the hit single by the Blackeyed Peas, "Let's Get It Started." While those of us professing Christ would seek to be disciples of Jesus and not simply follow our intuition, the point about breaking away from traditions that prevent us from becoming missional is essential. It is time for many African American congregations to recognize it is not enough to simply be the church. It is time to rethink the meaning of church for those who came after the civil rights struggle.

Some individuals probably have read all the chapters and are still not convinced. They are asking, **"Why should we rethink the meaning of church for post–civil rights generations?"** The simple answer is congregations who do not will continue to lose vitality and will eventually die. Another answer is because the ability to adapt and participate in God's work of transformation is a part of what has made the black church one of the most influential institutions in the United States.

Typically, African American congregations have rallied to fight a visible and definable other (e.g., racism). The challenge in this case is looking inward and seeking to transform what it means to be the church in a shifting culture. Both challenges are difficult, but looking inward is especially difficult because we perceive ourselves with prejudiced eyes. The reason things are not going well is always someone else's fault, never our own doing.

It is time to look in the mirror and not see dimly, but to be honest in the ways many of us have lost the ability to communicate the gospel in this shifting culture. I believe there is a hunger by many congregations to be vital again, to once again be sought by those in the community as a place where they can go to experience grace and start a journey toward wholeness.

Let's be honest: there is no quick fix! It is going to take a lot of work. All the evangelism programs in the world will not fix the current state of many African American congregations. The good news is many of these congregations can develop a new mindset that helps them to rethink the meaning of church for the post–civil rights generations. This book is just a first step in helping congregations to move forward in that process.

Congregations that develop a new mindset may never become megachurches, but they will be vital in their communities. These congregations will transform lives and society in new ways never imagined by their foreparents who left them a rich legacy. These congregations will redefine what it means to be the black church. Let's get it started!

GETTING STARTED

1. Congregations have to decide if they want to be vital. In Ezekiel (37:3), God asks, "Can these bones live?" Congregations that are committed to doing the same things, even when they are not working and not helping them discern the Spirit of God to lead them forward, are making a decision to die. The bones will

not live! If there is a willingness to live, then praying for God's direction is the first step. Please pray in a manner that you are seeking God's will and not trying to steer God in a particular direction. The whole congregation committing to pray for forty days and coming together to share how God spoke is one way to discern God's will. (Resource: Kevass J. Harding, *Can These Bones Live* [Nashville: Abingdon Press, 2007].)

2. Congregations have to start doing things differently. When the prodigal son realizes he has hit a low point in life (Luke 15:17-18), it is one thing to come to that realization, but another to do something about it. The prodigal son decides to return home. It is one thing for a congregation to realize a problem exists and to take the first step and pray. The rubber hits the road when God speaks and it requires the congregation to do things differently. For example, the Easter egg hunt gets moved to the community center so that others can participate. Congregations have to follow through and start doing things differently if they truly seek to be transformed. (Resource: Ralph C. Watkins, *The Gospel Remix: Reaching the Hip Hop Generation* [Valley Forge, Pa.: Judson Press, 2007].)

3. Congregations have to listen to those in the post–civil rights generations. Elisha tells Naaman (2 Kings 5:10-11) to go wash in the Jordan seven times and his leprosy will be cleansed, but Naaman initially walks away angry. Naaman did not listen to Elisha because he did not believe what he said had value. If congregations want to be transformed, then listening to voices that have an important message is necessary. A part of developing a new mindset is a willingness to listen. A willingness to listen will translate into individuals seeing and eventually experiencing a difference in your congregation. (Resource: Olu Brown, *From*

Zero to Eighty: Innovative Ideas for Planting and Accelerating Church Growth [Atlanta: Impact Press, 2010].

I have described all three of these ideas throughout the book, but highlighted them one more time as your congregation prepares for a new journey. This journey has no guarantees, but it is one that will help you to rethink your future in a changing world.

ACTIVITIES

1. Read Ezekiel 37:3. Develop a congregational prayer plan for discerning God's direction.

2. Read about the prodigal son in Luke 15. Name three church activities that can be done differently to include those in the community.

3. Read 2 Kings 5:10-11. Invite non-church individuals from the post–civil rights generations to share their understanding of God with you. This should be a time of listening and not trying to prove a point!

NOTES

Introduction

1. Tim Condor, *The Church in Transition* (Grand Rapids: Zondervan, 2006), 13.
2. B. Cosby, M. Taylor, A. Muhammed, J. Davis, "We Can Get Down." A Tribe Called Quest. *Midnight Marauders*. LP. Zomba Label Group Legacy, 1993.

1. Shifting Culture

1. I am not a sociologist, so my rethinking these categories is for the purpose of illustrating theological shifts.
2. William Strauss and Neil Howe, *Generations: The History of America's Future, 1584 to 2069* (New York: William Morrow and Company, 1991), 8.
3. Ibid., 279.
4. Ibid.
5. Ibid., 281.
6. Ibid., 280.
7. Ibid., 285.
8. Ibid., 282.
9. Ibid., 299.
10. Ibid.
11. Ibid., 301.
12. Ibid., 303.
13. Ibid., 304.
14. Ibid., 309.
15. Ibid., 317.
16. Ibid.
17. Ibid.
18. Ibid., 320.
19. Ibid., 337.

20. Ibid., 338.
21. Ibid.
22. Ibid., 335.
23. Ibid., 342.
24. Ibid.
25. Ibid., 350.
26. Ibid.
27. Ibid.
28. Stacey M. Floyd-Thomas, *Black Church Studies: An Introduction* (Nashville: Abingdon Press, 2007), 29.
29. This in no way detracts from Obama's historic election as president of the United States, but points to the reality of the number of leaders developed during this time.
30. Floyd-Thomas, *Black Church Studies*, 35.
31. Martin Luther King, Jr., "The American Dream," in *A Testament of Hope: The Essential Writings and Speeches of Martin Luther King, Jr.*, ed. James M. Washington (San Francisco: HarperSanFrancisco, 1986), 212.
32. Ibid.
33. Floyd-Thomas, *Black Church Studies*, 39.
34. http://cghs.dadeschools.net/african-american/twentieth_century/panthers.htm.
35. Floyd-Thomas, *Black Church Studies*, 39.
36. This in no way denies the reality of tensions in these neighborhoods that often led to violence.
37. In some sense this was the elephant in the room in the O. J. Simpson case. Did he really remember where he came from and who had helped him to make it? Because of his means had he forgotten his roots?
38. I am not demeaning the impact of the Nation of Islam by this statement.
39. Maurice Clarrett, who was a highly recruited running back for the Ohio State Buckeyes, is an example of someone who bought into the economic dream.
40. Election 2008: Second-largest youth voter turnout in American history, *The Tartan* (Carnegie Mellon, November 10, 2008).
41. Floyd-Thomas, *Black Church Studies*, 43.

2. Old Wineskins

1. *United Methodist Hymnal*, "We Shall Overcome" (Nashville: United Methodist Publishing House, 1996), 533.
2. Jason Richard Hunter, lyrics. "Verbs of Power." X Clan. *To the East: Blackwards*. CD. Fontana Island Label, 1990. http://www.lyricsmode.com/lyrics/x/x_clan/verbs_of_power.html. Accessed 7-8-2010.

3. The hope was that African Americans would not only achieve legal citizenship rights, but be treated as citizens in society.
4. Alonzo Washington in Kansas City is an example of such a person. He is the person that many seek when they are looking for a spokesperson.
5. Sam Cooke, "A Change Is Gonna Come." Sam Cooke. Abkco Music, Inc.
6. Read some of King's speeches and sermons and notice the way he weaves biblical imagery into both regardless of where he was speaking. One resource for this is A *Testament of Hope: The Essential Writings and Speeches of Martin Luther King, Jr.*, ed. James M. Washington (San Francisco: HarperSanFrancisco, 1986).
7. Moving forward in the book I will not address the issue of economic marginalization to a great extent, but it is important to put this issue on the table.

3. New Wineskins

1. Talib Kweli Greene, Weldon Irvine, Otis Jackson, Jr., Tommy Smith, "Eat to Live." Talib Kweli. *Eardrum*. CD. Blacksmith Records, 2007.
2. I am not speaking of simply numerical decline, but also spiritual decline.
3. Lauryn Hill, "I Get Out." Lauryn Hill. *Unplugged MTV*. CD. Columbia, 2002. .
4. Lawrence Parker, "The Truth." KRS-One. *KRS-One*. CD. Jive Records, 1995.
5. Jill Scott, "A Long Walk." Jill Scott. *Who Is Jill Scott? Words and Sounds*, Vol 1. CD. Hidden Beach, 2000.
6. Josef Sorett, "RZA's The Tao of Wu: Hip Hop Religion, Spiritual Sampling, and Race in a 'Post-Racial' Age," in *religion dispatches* (March 24, 2010).
7. Henry H. Mitchell, *Black Church Beginnings: The Long-Hidden Realities of the First Years* (Grand Rapids: William B Eerdmans Publishing Company, 2004), 3.
8. Damon Blackmon, Nasir Jones, "God Loves Us." Nasir Jones. *Nastradmus*. CD. Ill Will, 1999.
9 Yafeu Fula, Kotari Cox, Tyrone Wrice, Bruce Washington, Tupac Shakur, Joseph Paquette, Rufus Cooper, "Hail Mary." Tupac Shakur. *The Best of 2Pac—Part 1: Thug*. CD. Amaru, 2007.
10. Nina Simone, Talib Kweli Greene, Terrance Quaites, Kanye Omari West, "Listen." Talib Kweli. *Eardrum*. CD. Blacksmith Records, 2007. Read more: http://www.metrolyrics.com/listen-lyrics-talib-kweli.html#ixzz0yL88AKmz.
11. Drew Ramsey, India Arie Simpson, Shannon Sanders, "Better People." *Testimony, Vol. 1, Life and Relationships*. CD. Motown, 2006.
12. Mos Def, "There Is a Way." Mos Def. *True Magic*. Geffen, 2006.
13. Ibid.

4. New Wine

1. George Clinton, Gregory Jacobs, Bootsy Collins, Walter Morrison, "Humpty Dance." Digital Underground. *Sex Packets*. CD. Tommy Boy, 1990.
2. Leonard Sweet, *Postmodern Pilgrims*. Sweet uses the term *connectivity*, and I am adapting his use of this term. The phrase "connecting people with God" is a part of the Saint James UMC (Kansas City, Mo.) mission statement.

5. A Better Wineskin

1. India Arie, "India's Song." India Arie. *Testimony, Vol. 1, Life and Relationships*.
2. Congregations should consider including those homebound or nursing homebound in this ministry. We often send these individuals bulletins but do not include them in ministries of the church.
3. Martha Grace Reese, *Unbinding the Gospel: Real Life Evangelism* (St. Louis: Chalice Press, 2006), 46.

Conclusion

1. Will Adams, Allan Pineda, Jaime Gomez, Terence Yoshiaki, Michael Fratantuno, George Pajon Jr., "Let's Get It Started." Blackeyed Peas. *Elephunk*. CD. A&M Records, 2004.

STUDY GUIDE

New Wine New Wineskins is a six-week study (this can be shortened—see examples below). It is best done as a small group study (optimal number is from 10 to 12). The purpose is to help congregations connect with the post–civil rights generations who are often not as active in the church. This study will give participants new eyes for seeing opportunities in building bridges between generations in a way that maintains the integrity of the Gospel.

Resources
1. *New Wine New Wineskins*
2. Bible
3. Chart or board and writing utensils
4. Suggest reading or listening to some of the songs for applicable chapters

Options for Studying the Book
Six Weeks
Week 1—Introduction and chapter 1
Week 2—Chapter 2
Week 3—Chapter 3
Week 4—Chapter 4
Week 5—Chapter 5

Week 6—Conclusion
To do as a four-week study, combine chapters 2 and 3, combine 5
and the conclusion.

Suggested Format
A one-hour time limit is flexible depending on group.
1. Sharing congregational concerns for outreach   (5 minutes)
2. Opening prayer   (3 minutes)
3. Icebreaker (reading or listening to lyrics
   and writing words and images that stick out)   (5 minutes)
4. Scripture reading (under activity section at end
   of each chapter)   (12 minutes)
5. Discuss group questions (end of chapters)   (30 minutes)
6. Closing prayer   (5 minutes)

Helpful Hints
1. Session leader should be prepared!
2. Affirm questions and responses so that individuals feel like
   they are valued contributors. It also important to make sure
   one or two voices do not dominate the conversation.
3. Determine ahead of time if food and drinks will be a part of
   the study. Have these set up in advance.
4. Have fun!